The Dick Myers Project

by

Seth Shaffer

Copyright © 2017 by Seth Shaffer
All Rights Reserved. No part of this book may be reproduced in any form or by any electronic or mechanical means, including information storage and retrieval systems, without permission in writing from the publisher, except by reviewers who may quote brief passages in a review.

Library and Archives Canada Cataloguing in Publication

Shaffer, Seth, author
    The Dick Myers project / by Seth Shaffer.

ISBN 978-0-921845-45-4 (softcover)

    1. Myers, Dick. 2. Puppeteers--United States--Biography.
3. Puppet theater--United States--History. 4. Puppet making--
United States--History. I. Title.

PN1982.M94S53 2017   791.5'3092   C2017-903609-2

Front Cover Photograph:
Minstrel from *Beauty and the Beast*.
Courtesy Elizabeth Shaffer.

Charlemagne Press
Garden Bay, BC
V0N 1S1 Canada
www.charlemagnepress.com

Contents

	Foreword by Bart Roccoberton	v
	Preface	vii
	Introduction	ix
	Photo Credits	xii
1	The Early Years: 1921-1966	1
2	Limelight: 1966 - 1983	21
3	Retirement: 1983 - 2005	47
4	Myers Mechanics	55
5	Restoration	69
6	Exhibit	97
7	Rehearsals and Performances	113
8	Project Review	133
9	Scripts:	
	Dick Whittington	137
	Cinderella	150
	Beauty and the Beast	167
	Simple Simon	183

Richard (Dick) Myers
1921 - 2005

Foreword

Seth Shaffer was accepted into the graduate-level Puppet Arts Program at the University of Connecticut in 2010. He came to us with an undergraduate degree in theatre and film, as well as several years of experience as a puppeteer with Kids on the Block and Madcap Productions. He enthusiastically immersed into our classes and productions while helping the Ballard Institute and Museum of Puppetry (BIMP) digitize the Puppeteers of America's video archives. Working with this collection and meeting the frequent Puppetry dignitaries who visit the Puppet Arts Program and BIMP, Seth was inspired to learn as much as possible about the history of American Puppetry and its many participants and attributes.

Among the masters' names he heard frequently was that of Dick Myers. Seth also had the opportunity to see and examine some of the Myers puppets which are on display in the UConn Puppet Arts Complex. As his interest in Myers grew, Seth became aware of a challenge that had been presented to me by Allelu Kurten and Dick Myers, himself. It intrigued him.

I had come to know Dick in the mid-1970s, when I was a graduate student in the UConn Puppetry Program. Albrecht Roser, Margo Rose and Allelu Kurten introduced us. Dick became a frequent guest in our home and would often go out with us for performances of The Pandemonium Puppet Company (Brad Williams, Rachel Prescott, Marge Roccoberton and myself). At the same time we were learning from this international master, Dick was studying us and asking many questions. I will always remember him sitting on the floor listening to albums on our stereo with a small notebook in hand to jot down ideas inspired by the music.

Dick Myers had toured across North America, Europe, Russia and Japan. He was renowned as a solo puppeteer who worked to a pre-recorded soundtrack which he could manipulate in order to respond in real time to his audience. His apparently simple geometric-shaped puppets had both dramatic depth and comic life, and the clever mechanisms crafted through his skills as an aeronautics engineer were unique. Add to that a dry mid-western sense of humor and you can gain a sense of the success of his productions, internationally. However, in all of his travels his shows were never documented on film or video. Nancy Staub had invited him to perform at the 1980 World Puppet Festival in Washington, D.C., which was co-hosted by UNIMA-U.S.A. and the Puppeteers of America. Working with WQED in Pittsburgh, Jim Henson video-documented every performance at the event. Unfortunately, Dick chose to tour Ireland instead.

As his health was failing in 2005, Allelu Kurten convinced Dick his legacy had the chance to be upheld if he would give all of his shows to me. With his agreement, I was charged with remounting the shows and having them video documented for posterity.

In two large vans, Larry Engler and I brought all of Dick's puppets, sets, props and show tapes back to the University of Connecticut. The first quest was to digitize the 35 year-old reel-to-reel tapes. I received a Dean's Grant from the School of Fine Arts and we were able to have the tapes digitally reproduced. The next challenge was to find the right person, or persons, who could respectfully remount the shows.

That person proved to be Seth Shaffer. In my Trends in Contemporary American Puppetry class, Seth continued to demonstrate a strong interest in the ways Puppetry has developed in the U.S. Learning of the challenge that Allelu had brought to me with the Myers collection, Seth asked if the remounting of the shows would be a worthy MFA Project. It surely was, and after some consideration, we decided Seth should focus on *Cinderella* and *Beauty and the Beast* (Allelu's favorites).

As he pulled together the various pieces of the two shows, Seth started to research Dick Myers' life and career. When he discovered how little had been written about Dick and his shows, Seth realized he would need to interview people who knew Dick and had seen his performances.

The remounting of the two shows was remarkable. Without question, Seth honored Dick Myers' memory and his creativity with performances were equal to Dick's own efforts. Of course, using Dick's show tapes, the master's voice was fully present, in addition to his booth, his sets and his unique puppets. However, these remountings would have had little effect if it were not for Seth Shaffer's respect and talent. Both shows have now been performed many times and they have been digitally documented.

This publication you are now reading is the result of Seth's research about Dick Myers. In addition to production, a Summary Book detailing the process and results of the project is part of the requirements of an MFA in Puppet Arts at the University of Connecticut. Seth included his research on Dick Myers. As I read it, I learned many things that I had never known about my friend, Dick Myers, and recommended Seth consider publishing. I am very happy Luman Coad and Charlemagne Press have agreed.

It is my hope that, in the near future, Seth Shaffer will be able to work on remounting Dick Myers' *Dick Whittington* and *Simple Simon*.

Bart. P. Roccoberton, Jr.
Director, Puppet Arts Program
University of Connecticut

Preface

This book began in 2011, when I started researching the work of Dick Myers. I first became aware of Myers' work while attending a class on American puppet history at the University of Connecticut. My professor, Bart Roccoberton Jr., tasked us to research and write a biography on different American puppeteers and puppetry movements. As he discussed Myers' work, and demonstrated a Myers' puppet, I was fascinated. Roccoberton said Myers would be tough puppeteer to research. His work was not documented in one easily accessible source, but thinly spread throughout modern puppet history, and the memories of an aging generation of puppeteers.

While at the time I did not take on the challenge of researching Myers' life, the curiosity stirred within me. Soon after, I began working at the Ballard Institute and Museum of Puppetry archives. I found myself immersed long past my work hours reading and researching about the path many puppeteers before me had taken. And of course, I still had a strong curiosity about who was this enigma of a man Dick Myers.

The archives at the Ballard Institute and Museum of Puppetry are a puppetry historian's dreamland. The archives house a large collection of books on puppetry, a complete set of Puppetry Journals, the paper and correspondence collection of Marjorie Batchelder-McPharlin, correspondence to and from Margo and Rufus Rose, and correspondence to and from Frank Ballard, to name a few. The largest asset to this project was the Rose correspondence. It led me on the historical journey of Myers' early career in puppetry.

This book could not have been completed without the help of many amazing and kindhearted people. The Dick Myers Project would have not been possible without the support and encouragement of several people. I would like to take this opportunity to thank everyone who helped me along the way of this project. First, I would like to thank Bart P. Roccoberton Jr. for his commitment and support in helping make this project a success. Not only did Roccoberton provide dedication to advising and directing these shows, but he also shaped me to be the puppeteer that I am.

Other great mentors both on this project and while attending graduate school include: Paul Spirito, Dr. John Bell, Vincent Cardinal, and Laura Crow. Additionally, I would like to thank Ronnie Burkett, Paul Vincent Davis, Johan Vandergun, Luman Coad, Penny Francis, Ray DiSilva, Alan Cook, Phillip Huber, Steven Abrams, Richard Termine, Marilyn Miller, Fred Thompson, Michael Graham, Bob Howard, Bob Nathanson, Elise Handelman, Tom Bonham, Nancy Staub, Paul Mesner, Paul Eide, and Gary Busk for all of their great insight and information into Myers' work.

I would especially like to thank Allelu Kurten for all of her dedication to Myers during his lifetime and afterwards. I am so greatly honored to have had the opportunity to hear wonderful stories from Allelu about not only Dick Myers, but also about her own career and journey as a puppeteer. Without Allelu, this project would never have happened. Furthermore, I would like to thank Dana Samborski for his hard work in mold making, Carianne Hoff for her talented painting skills, Barbara Zizka for her dedication to transcribing Dick Myers' audio tapes, Sarah Nolen for her amazing photography, and Xing Xin Liu for her help during the CRT and National Festival performances. Also, I would like to thank Madeleine Smith for assistance in editing this book.

Finally, I would like to thank my wife Elizabeth Shaffer for her loving devotion to both the success of this project and myself as an artist. Thank you for all that you do! Thank you everyone!

Photo Credits

Ballard Institute and Museum of Puppetry
1, 7, 8

Phillip Huber
18

Myers Document Archives
iv, 9, 11, 12, 13, 14, 15, 17, 18, 19, 20, 21, 23, 25, 26, 33, 34, 35, 36, 37, 49, 50, 54, 107, 108

Sarah Nolen
31, 32, 42, 43, 45, 46, 47, 48, 95, 96, 104

Production Stills (from Video)
33, 105, 106

Puppetry Journal
2, 3, 4

Bart Roccoberton
16

Rose Archives & Z. Briggs
6

Elizabeth Shaffer
5, 10, 22, 24, 27, 28, 29, 30, 39, 40, 78, 79, 80, 81, 82, 83, 84, 85, 86, 87, 88, 89, 90, 91, 92, 93, 94, 97, 98, 99, 100, 101, 102, 103, 109, 110, 111, 112, 113

Seth Shaffer
41, 51, 52, 53, 55, 56, 57, 58, 59, 60, 61, 62, 63, 64, 65, 66, 67, 68, 69, 70, 71, 72, 73, 74, 75, 76, 77

David Stephens
41

www.artsdelamarionette.eu
114

Introduction

Audience members enter the theatre. A puppet booth is set in the center of the stage. A bright blue cyclorama is glowing brilliantly. The only thing on the puppet stage: a red ball. The audience is rustling, chatting in their seats, waiting with much anticipation of the show they are about to watch. Whether it was their first or seventh time watching this performance, they all are filled with the same anticipation.

The house lights go down; the audience quiets slightly, as they finish their last few comments. In the now darkened theatre, the only light to be seen is the bright blue cyclorama; blazing even more brilliantly than before. Finally, there is movement on the puppet stage. The bright red ball, now in silhouette, slowly and smoothly rolls off. The audience is silent.

Elegantly and with charm, music begins to fill the air. Slowly, the silhouettes of the first scene move onto the stage like clockwork. The puppet booth lights come up and reveal to the audience the interior of a house: Cinderella's house. The Narrator's voice sets the scene, informing the audience this is the miserable home where Cinderella lives with her two evil stepsisters. The narration is taken over by music as we hear a click-clack-click-clack sound as Cinderella enters to clean the house. Soon, she is joined by her

loving companion, Fred the Mouse. Together, they whimsically dance as they clean, which creates a loving and poetic scene.

This is what it would have been like to see Dick Myers' *Cinderella* in performance. Myers was a puppet cultural phenomenon who seemed to blossom overnight once he created his first solo rod puppet show, *Dick Whittington and His Cat.* This book seeks to outline his career and life in a comprehensive way. Myers was a social recluse outside of his performances; he lived a life of solidarity, while living on the kindness of those around him.

Throughout, this book provides not only a look at the process of the Dick Myers Project, but also explores the steps taken to restore his shows and puppets, and offers a look back to some of his performances. Myers' last performance that I have been able to find documentation was given in 1983, the same year I was born. How could a young performer recreate work of a performer he never met and shows he never saw (shows that had no video documentation)? It was a long and rewarding process resulting in this book. I do not attempt to tell an idealized story of Myers' life, but instead tell the story of his life (good and bad) as I have been able to piece it together. Included in this book, I share my own journey in the restoration and remounting of these historical puppet shows.

Early Years

1921-1966

When I began the process of remounting Dick Myers' puppet shows, I knew it could not be taken lightly and would require much research. A puppeteer's work is made from materials and passion, and serves not only as an art form, but also as an extension of the artist himself. I approached the Dick Myers Project as an opportunity to uncover the history of a genius, whose work and life experiences were fading memories in an already aging generation of puppeteers. My research combines written accounts of Myers' work (from the varying perspectives of observers and Myers himself), as well as recollections from the memories of his friends and peers. These accounts do not always hold Myers in the best of light, but they are essential in painting a portrait of this eccentric man and a true genius of the puppet theatre.

Richard (Dick) Milo Myers was born at Hurley Hospital in Flint, Michigan on May 21, 1921 at 2:00 p.m. His father was Richard R. Myers, a mechanical dentist whose specialty was engineering and fitting dental implants. Dick's mother, Mabel (Primley) Myers, was a housewife. Although both Richard and his wife Mabel were from Elkhart, Indiana, at the time of Dick's birth, they resided at 722 Wolcott Street in Flint, Michigan; a residence only two

Fig. 1. Backstage during Rufus and Margo Rose's production of *Dick Whittington and His Cat*.

blocks from the hospital where Dick was born. The family's stay in Michigan would be short lived. They soon moved to 1425 East Jackson Blvd in Elkhart, Indiana, where they would raise their two children, Dick and his sister Marietta.

While attending grade school in Elkhart, Dick Myers watched his first puppet show, *Dick Whittington and His Cat* by Rufus and Margo Rose (Fig. 1).[1] For Myers, this production sparked an immediate love for the art form and would later inspire his career path. At age seventeen, Myers set out to learn and experience more about puppetry by traveling to Middlebury, Indiana. Once there, he met with Martin and Olga Stevens, nationally renowned husband and wife puppeteers, who immediately made friends with Myers and allowed him to help around their puppet studio, called The Mousetrap.[2] The tasks Myers undertook are unknown.

However, it can be said this experience proved to instill in him a lifelong passion for the puppet theatre.

After working briefly for Stevens Puppets, Myers decided to seek out a college education. He pursued a degree in engineering from Tri-State College (now Trine University) in Angola, IN, and found his engineering skills would be an asset to the Navy[3]. Myers did not spend much time in the Navy before returning to his true passions: puppetry and theatre. In an interview with the *Elkhart Truth*, Myers was quoted, "When I came home from service […] I wanted to get into theater"[4]. He did just that.

Myers studied drama at the Goodman Theatre, which at the time was part of the Chicago Art Institute. He studied every aspect of theatre, with the hope of learning the necessary techniques for creating a great show. When not in classes, Myers travelled around the Chicago area on behalf of the Good Teeth Council for Children.[5] During this tour, he used hand puppets to teach dental health to audiences of all ages.[6] Soon after, Myers studied fine art at both Washington University and the University of Cincinnati.[7] While he gained a wide variety of skills from each of the three educational facilities he attended, he did not receive a degree from any of them.

The year 1946 came to be of great significance for Myers. After returning to Elkhart, Indiana, he rekindled a friendship and professional relationship with Martin and Olga Stevens, and in 1946, he joined the national puppetry organization, Puppeteers of America.[8] He also attended and volunteered at the 1946 Puppetry Festival at the home of Rufus and Margo Rose in Waterford, Connecticut[9]. Myers must have been very excited to once again see the puppeteers who first sparked his interest in the puppet theatre. Although his duties at the festival are unclear, it is evident he helped significantly because he was thanked in the *Grapevine* (a national publication on puppetry that was published every two months by Paul McPharlin). Martin Stevens had thought Myers to be "very capable" and in 1947 sent him out to represent the

Stevens Marionettes as a second touring branch of his company.[10]

What this second touring branch would entail was not clear until 1947, when Dick Myers and Eunice Smith presented *This Funny World*, a script by Martin Stevens. The puppetry community saw the production on June 27, 1947 at 8:30 p.m., right before Burr Tillstrom's (creator of the television show *Kukla, Fran and Ollie*) production of *St. George and the Dragon* at the National Puppetry Festival in St. Louis, Missouri.[11] A note on this production provides an exciting landscape of the show:

Fig. 2. Gigi and Blow from Stevens' *This Funny World*.

A good crowd gathered in the Bishop Tuttle Auditorium on Friday evening for a double bill with performances by the Stevens' Marionettes and Burr Tillstrom.

The Stevens' production of *"This Funny World"* was presented first. Puppeteers Dick [Myers] and Eunice Smith did an admirable job from the bridge. An unusual type of open front stage was used for this production. The scenic problems of this type of stage were solved with the use of painted drops behind velvet masking with a large circular cut-out. Between acts the lights were switched from stage to bridge. While Dick announced the next number, a drop was released and when the lights were switched back to the stage, the audience was surprised to find that a change of scenery had taken place while their attention had been focused onto the puppeteers.

The show concerned the adventures of Mr. G.I. who was incidentally a portrait puppet of Dick [Myers]. Mr. G.I. was in search of talent for a show. Each scene showed him in a different country as he conducted his search. One of the top laughs was in the Australian act when Mother Kangaroo told Junior Kangaroo to stop stamping his feet. In the Egyptian number an ostrich laid an egg. The egg broke open and out popped three little ostriches who did a chorus routine. The show ended in a patriotic vein with Mr. G.I. returning to the U.S.A. Mr. G.I. met the Statue of Liberty in front of a scene showing the skyline of New York with the clouds worked into a flag effect.

The show was very well received and everyone agreed that the Stevens had again demonstrated their ability to produce excellent shows with a wide range of versatility.[12]

This Funny World provided puppeteers with a great first impression of Myers as not only a performer, but also as a sound equipment technician and creator. Though this show was a success among puppeteers, communities, and schools, very few of the puppets from this production have survived. One of the infamous puppets from the show was a topless female dancer named "Gigi".[13] (Fig. 2) Though this production was toured and performed primarily in schools around the US, Gigi was never removed from the show. At the time, the puppet's nudity was

not an issue because she was considered to be from an "exotic," "primitive" nation. Another infamous puppet from the show was Mr. G.I., the only puppet ever modeled after Dick Myers. Unfortunately, there are no photos showing the design of this puppet, which has yet to be found.

Rounding off the 1947 festival, Myers gave a five-minute workshop titled, "What to Do When Your Sound Equipment Fails." This workshop was offered for five minutes, from 12:25 pm-12:30 pm.[14] Myers was a technological genius, but with a five-minute workshop, it is unclear what he could have demonstrated. He might have told everyone, when a sound system fails, one needs to talk louder.

In 1947, Myers' technological skills were put to the test in a new Stevens' Marionettes production of *Taming of the Shrew*. For the production, Myers built a switchboard. Impressed with Myers' skills, Martin Stevens wrote a letter of praise of Myers' work, which would be featured in *The Grapevine Telegraph*. The letter stated, "Dick Myers built a gorgeous new switchboard [...] and might be induced to build your new switch board [*sic*] if you'd write him".[15] Myers also built the sound system for *This Funny World*, a skill he would continue to refine his entire life. Martin Stevens included in a letter to Margo and Rufus Rose:

> True Dick built the original sound system for *Funny World* of such proportions that after he got through tearing it down and making it over, we had enough used material left to build our new theatre in Tuscany, but that's a savings with building costs what they are.[16]

While Myers worked with the Stevens, he began developing a new style of rod puppet with intricate mechanisms to control the puppet's movements. As his technological advancements progressed, he searched for independence as a performer. At the time, rod puppetry was a mostly underexplored area of puppetry in America. Myers' exploration of the rod puppet was progressive;

however, he did not at the time fully understand its abilities. In fact, one unfinished rod puppet lay on a desk at The Mousetrap for months before Myers finished it. Martin Stevens demanded Myers paint the puppet, or else Stevens would paint it for him. Although Myers did have a finished rod puppet in the late 1940s, he would not fully understand its role on his career until two decades later.

By August of 1947, Myers was no longer performing in the Stevens' *This Funny World*, and was replaced by George Latshaw.[17] Myers had taken leave from *This Funny World* to further his knowledge on the quickly advancing technologies of the motion picture world. He found employment with a New York City firm that made both sound equipment and motion picture cameras.[18] He worked hard to become a proficient cameraman and began to learn more about sound engineering. Both skills would prove to be very useful in Myers' lifetime.

By late 1947, Myers had earned the respect of Rufus and Margo Rose, and was invited to perform in their production of *A Christmas Carol*.[19] Myers' primary role in the production had been to serve as a technical crewmember. For this position, he managed the lighting and the sound effects, and assisted with puppet wrangling. Additionally, he performed a few of the puppets in the show; he performed Bob Cratchet (manipulating the puppet, but not voicing it) at the beginning of the show and later performed the Yellow Girl during the Fezziewig scene. Myers also performed the mechanical version of Big Ben. Rufus and Margo Rose had three assistants on this film: Myers and two of the Roses' sons, Jim and Rufus Jr. (a.k.a. Bunny).

The production was not only a public show offered in the Roses' theatre in Waterford, CT, but it also became the first live broadcast of a full-length puppet production in television history.[20] It is unclear whether Myers was a part of this television broadcast, which aired on WJZ-TV, the American Broadcast Company in Chicago. On December 24, 1948, the show was presented under

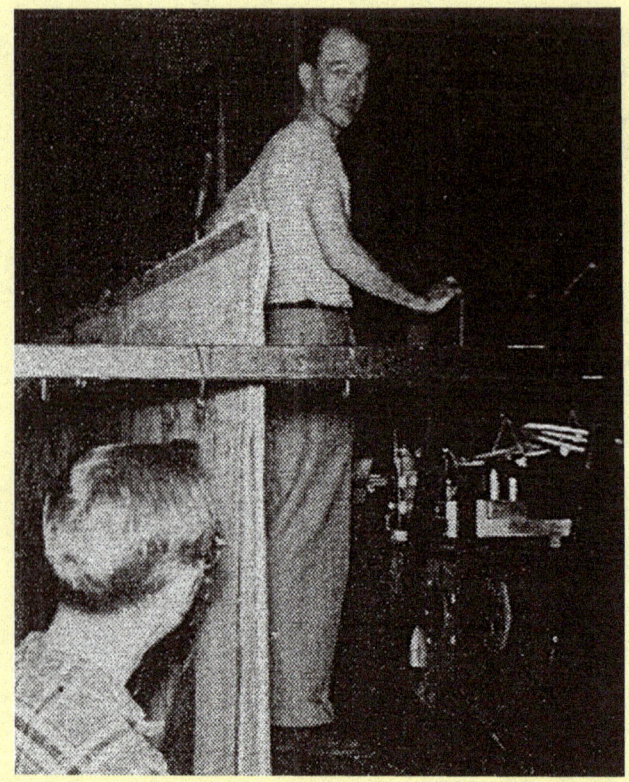

Fig. 3. Fay Coleman (*on bridge*) and Dick Myers (*forefront*) backstage rehearsal of *Tom Sawyer*.

the title, *Scrooge*. Rufus Rose had hoped *Christmas Carol* would be a yearly television event, but the show was only presented on the air for one season.

Impressed with Myers' quality of work, Rufus Rose continued to employ him. In 1948, Rose sent Myers and puppeteer Kent More out to perform one-man hand puppet shows. These shows served as a form of advertising for the Roses' work.[21] There are no clear records of what these shows would have been like, as no puppets, records, or scripts have survived. This did, however, spark a brief professional relationship between More and Myers. In December of 1948, Myers joined Kent and Louis More in New York City. Myers was the stage manager of their production of *King Midas*, presented through New York's Children's World Theatre.[22]

While in New York City, Myers continued to study camera, sound, and lighting techniques and advancements. On June 30, 1949, both Dick Myers and Ed Johnson gave a stage lighting demonstration at the National Puppetry Festival in Detroit,

Michigan.[23] This 45-minute demonstration was a perfect opportunity for Myers to share his knowledge of electronics and stage lighting. His hard work ethic would continue to be noticed by many. Notably, Myers worked with Fay Coleman (a well-known Midwestern puppeteer) starting in 1949 and continued working for him until 1950 (Fig. 3). It is unknown as to why Myers' service with Coleman ended. However, it is known that in February of 1950, Roy Etherington took over the position Myers once had.[24] Reflecting on the matter, Martin Stevens wrote:

> The enclosed letter is from Dick, and I think it is funny enough to pass on to you. Throw it away. Haven't talked with him at length yet, but they got someone from Detroit to finish out the season with Coleman, so that's good.[25]

That letter by Myers has yet to be found, but it can be said Myers' termination brought an end to a once close partnership. Later, Stevens would write, "Ah yes – Myers. Bless his heart. I dunno; but God does".[26]

After the end of his employment with Coleman, Myers returned home to Elkhart, Indiana. Around the same time, Martin and Olga Stevens were in a horrible car accident, leaving both puppeteers very banged up, and without a car. Physically incapable of doing the tour alone, the Stevens called on Myers to assist them on the road. In a letter to the Roses, Olga explained:

> When we got back to Middlebury, our friends wanted to take us in, so we ain't been home yet. Then a card [came] from Dick before he knew about our accident saying he was coming home. Then another after he knew saying he was a good nurse and carrier of wood. We just talked with him on the phone and he will get our new car (as soon as the man gets a rack to hold the load back, installed) and drive us up to Grand Rapids to our doctor friend for a good looking over. Then, beginning next Friday, he will go with us on our dates and do the heavy work.[27]

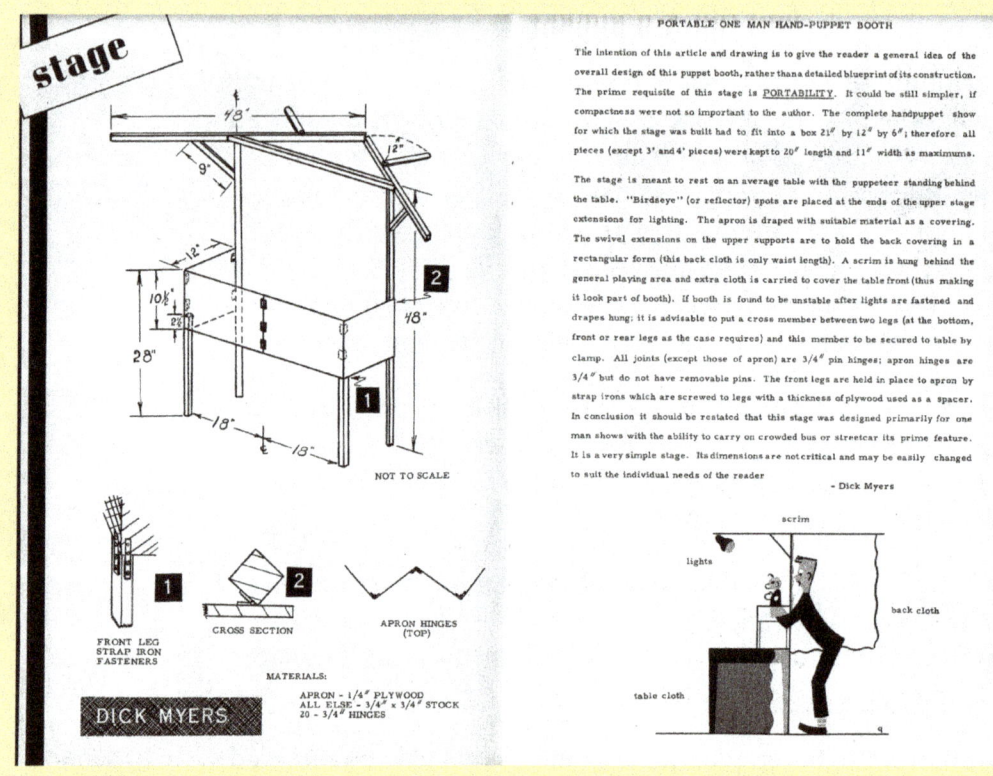

Fig. 4. "Portable One Man Hand-Puppet Booth" by Dick Myers.

Fig. 5. Puppets from *The Magic Potion* by Dick Myers.

Myers' work on the tour would prove to be of great help for the Stevens. As Martin Stevens explained in the *Puppetry Journal*:

> Dick Myers "saved our lives" after our recent smash-up by driving for us, setting up, tearing down, loading and unloading our equipment, and helping tremendously during our *Passion Play* dates.[28]

Through his willingness and dedication to help fellow puppeteers, Myers truly had created for himself a prime network. Though Myers had worked for many successful puppet theatres, he longed for something more.

Myers enjoyed working with other puppeteers (most of the time), but he had a desire to develop a one-man show. Myers wrote an article for the newly-formed national puppetry magazine, *The Puppetry Journal* in 1949, discussing his plans for building a hand puppet booth.[29] (Fig. 4) This was one of the few articles he would ever write for the public. With the help of Martin Stevens, Myers went to work on creating the small one-man hand puppet show. The hand puppets were primarily made of fabric, and were soft sculpted, darted, sewn, and stuffed to create the different characters of Myers' first script, *The Magic Potion* (Fig. 5). After building this show, Myers determined he did not wish to work with fabric again.[30] Prior to the premiere of *The Magic Potion* at the 1950 National Puppetry Festival in Oxford, Ohio, Myers gave a performance to Martin and Olga Stevens. Martin wrote in the *Puppetry Journal*, "He [Myers] is now readying his new hand puppet show, which will really be a treat for you at the Festival. We've just seen a preview!"[31] After the successful performance at the National Puppetry Festival, Myers was invited to perform *The Magic Potion* at a post-festival function called the 1950 Institute. This function, like the festival, was held at Western College (now Miami University) in Oxford, Ohio.[32] During the Christmas season of 1951, Myers performed *The Magic Potion* several times throughout his hometown of Elkhart, Indiana[33]. Afterwards,

Fig. 6. (*Left*) Chris Rose and Dick Myers.

Fig 7 & 8. (*Right & Below*)
Dick Whittington and His Cat puppets during construction.

he left performing on the stage to begin working on his other passions: audio-visual technology.

In 1949, the Stevens-Rose Puppet Film Company was established, and Myers was hired to work on two Stevens-Rose puppet films. This new puppet film company had noticed Myers' explorations of cinematography, sound, and lighting for the camera. These explorations had provided him with a high level of technical competency. Each film would be created at the Rose's home/studio in Waterford, Connecticut. The first film Myers assisted on was an adaptation of a hand puppet show called, *The Toymaker*, written by Martin Stevens. Primarily, his tasks for the profit after expenses.[36] Due to the small amount of income from the film and the lack of mass distribution, there were limited prints made of *The Toymaker* and *The Ant and the Grasshopper*. Currently, there is a print of *The Toymaker* in the collection of the Ballard Institute and Museum of Puppetry in Storrs, Connecticut. Unfortunately, there are no known prints of *The Ant and the Grasshopper*. What remains are photographs capturing the hard work and dedication which went into creating these films. After he had devoted three years to creating puppet films, Myers sought out new employment.

To pay his bills, Myers found work wherever he could. On April 18, 1951, Rufus Rose had written in a letter to Martin Stevens:

> Dick Myers has been with us for the past few days. Left this forenoon for Woodstock, New York to get a job as a waiter #3 in the greasy spoon there. He don't know what he's after but he's gettin' by and havin' fun. His job at Maurer's petered out through reorganization or sumpin'.

Although Myers had not found work in the puppetry field, he did find employment that enabled him to further perfect his endeavors in filmmaking. Myers began working for an industrial film production company called Bert Johnston Productions (later a part of Crosely Corporation) in Cincinnati, Ohio. While there, Myers

proved to be a competent cameraman, sound engineer, lighting designer, and film editor.³⁷

By 1956, Myers returned to Woodstock, New York, and established a puppetry studio called Puppet Arts. It was set up inside of a cabin that was rent-free as long as he kept the alcohol distilling and turned the alcohol bottles a quarter turn every week. Here, Myers continued to build a show with the unique rod puppet style he began to develop years before at The Mousetrap. The show he was writing and building was *Dick Whittington and His Cat* (his unique script was based off the first puppet show he ever watched). (Fig. 7 & 8) It is unclear whether he performed this show in these early years, or whether he just continued to develop it until it was perfect. Myers did receive the Woodstock Foundation Award for artistic endeavor while living in Woodstock, however, he once again had trouble marketing himself and had to seek additional work outside of puppetry.

Fig. 9. Dick Myers with his personal airplane.

Around 1960, Myers put aside his puppets and moved to Boston, Massachusetts, where he put an ad in the *New York Times* and found a job as a photographer for the government. During his employment, Myers had the extraordinary opportunity to photograph one of the early Discover missions (a missile that was launched into space and successfully returned). In an interview, Myers discussed his photography:

> I got the job of photographing at night one of the first missiles that ever went out into outer space and came back. And we recovered it. So they brought it into Boston and I set my cameras up: 35 [mm] and 16[mm]. I wasn't happy with the lights. I had [brought] big lights down to photograph this thing that had been brought in from outer space. So I looked around for a piece of paper…and I found just the right shade and the right everything. So I sat it down on one of the workbenches there and I photographed it on this little piece of paper. Went home and slept well. And when I came back in the morning, people were buzzing. "Did you hear, did you know that…they sent this missile into outer space and when it came back, it had silver on it!" And the people were [excited]. And I said, "oh my god, I did it again! This is my fault!" Because, what I did was the paper I picked up was photography paper, which is filled with silver. I put it down, and the heat from those lamps impregnated the [missile] and I had to go into the head boss and say, "Sorry, don't get too excited".[38]

Over the next several years, Myers explored aeronautical engineering in Boston and found work as an airline pilot, flight instructor, and a certified airplane mechanic (Fig. 9). In late 1965, the Stevens wrote: "Dick Myers, long since lost to puppetry, has completed achieving government licensing and gone west to have his own flying field".[39] Myers discussed what happened next in an interview:

> So I started with nothing [meaning skills in flight training] and worked my way through all the different pilot's exams and tests. Before I left this part of the country [New England] I got my mechanic's license too. That took another two years. And I decided to go to California and open a little airport. I had this little airplane. But when I landed at each little airport, I'd say I want to open [an airport] or buy land. I didn't have any money. And they'd say, "Look, land is so valuable out here that I could sell this little bit of land and retire for the rest of my life." Nothing worked out, so I flew this little airplane all the way back.[40]

Though Myers had some success with aeronautical work, he soon found himself wanting to return to puppetry.

In 1966, Myers was ready to get back into puppetry. He named his first solo company Puppet Arts of Woodstock, NY. Myers applied to the 1966 National Puppetry Festival in San Diego, California. He proposed to perform his show, *Dick Whittington and His Cat.* For Myers, this proved to be a very wise choice. With this single performance, Dick Myers would begin on a journey towards distinguished recognition in the field of puppetry around the world.

---

[1] Fulmer, Marcia. "Puppet Pioneer." *Elkhart Truth* [Indiana] 12 Nov. 1998: 1.

[2] Kashosravi, Cambiz, Dir. *Dick Myers: Master Puppeteer*. Perf. Dick Myers, Cambiz, 2004. DVD.

[3] Salter, Ted. "Caricature of the Month: Dick Myers." *Puppetry Journal* 29.2 (1977): 38.

[4] Fulmer, Marcia. "Puppet Pioneer." *Elkhart Truth* [Indiana] 12 Nov. 1998: 1

[5] Kashosravi, Cambiz, Dir. *Dick Myers: Master Puppeteer*. Perf. Dick Myers, Cambiz, 2004. DVD.

[6] Kashosravi, Cambiz, Dir. *Dick Myers: Master Puppeteer*. Perf. Dick Myers, Cambiz, 2004. DVD.

[7] Fulmer, Marcia. "Puppet Pioneer." *Elkhart Truth* [Indiana] 12 Nov. 1998: 1

[8] Batchelder, Marjorie H. "Current Members of Puppeteers of America." *The Grapevine Telegraph* 41 (1946): 14.

[9] Rose, Rufus. "A Message from Rufus Rose the Festival Chairman." *The Grapevine Telegraph* 42 (1946): 2.

[10] Wallace, Alfred. "Under the Bridge." *The Grapevine Telegraph* 43 (1946): 4.

[11] The Puppet Guild of St. Louis, ed. "1947 National Puppetry Festival." *The Grapevine Telegraph* 46 (1947): 26.

[12] Johnson, Edward. "Friday Evening June 27." *The Grapevine Telegraph.* 46 (1947): 40.

[13] Stevens, Olga. *Gigi and Blow by Olga and Martin Stevens.* 1950 *Puppetry Journal.* Ed. Vivian Michael. Vol.2. N 10.

[14] The Puppet Guild of St. Louis, ed. "1947 National Puppetry Festival." *The Grapevine Telegraph* 46 (1947) 27.

[15] Stevens, Martin. "Under the Bridge" *The Grapevine Telegraph* 47, 6.

[16] Stevens, Martin. Letter to Margo & Rufus Rose. 22 Nov. 1947. Middlebury, IN.

[17] Stevens, Martin. "Under the Bridge" *The Grapevine Telegraph* 48, 7.

[18] Fulmer, Marcia. "Puppet Pioneer." *Elkhart Truth* [Indiana] 12 Nov. 1998: 1.

[19] Stevens, Martin. "Under the Bridge" *The Grapevine Telegraph* 49, 7.

[20] Rose, Rufus. Letter to Martin Stevens, 17 Dec. 1948. Waterford. CT.

[21] Stevens, Martin. "Under the Bridge" *The Grapevine Telegraph* 49, 7.

[22] Stevens, Martin. "Under the Bridge" *The Grapevine Telegraph* 49, 7.

[23] Latshaw, George. "The Puppeteers of America National Puppetry Festival." *The Grapevine Telegraph.* 55 (1949): 18.

[24] Stevens, Martin. "Under the Bridge" *Puppetry Journal* 1.5 (1950): 4.

[25] Stevens, Martin. Letter to Rufus Rose. 6 March, 1950. Middlebury, IN.

[26] Stevens, Martin. Letter to Rufus Rose. 23 April, 1951. Middlebury, IN.

[27] Stevens, Martin. Letter to Rufus & Margo Rose. 6 March, 1950. Middlebury, IN.

[28] Stevens, Martin. "Under the Bridge" *Puppetry Journal* 1.6 (1950): 6.

[29] Myers. Dick. "Portable One Man Hand-puppet Booth." *Puppetry Journal* 1.4 (1949): 10-11.

[30] Kurten, Allelu. "The Life of Dick Myers Interview with Allelu Kurten." Personal interview. 6 Dec. 2012.

[31] Stevens, Martin "Under the Bridge" *Puppetry Journal* 1.6, 6.

[32] Rose, Margo. "Puppetry Institute." *Puppetry* Journal 2.1 (1950): 5.

[33] Stevens, Martin. "Under the Bridge" *Puppetry Journal* 2.4 (1951): 21.

[34] Stevens, Martin. "Under the Bridge" *Puppetry Journal* 2.6, (1951): 22.

[35] Stevens, Martin. *Martin Stevens: His* Book. Ed. Luman Coad. N.p. Charlemagne, 2002: 101.

[36] Rose, Rufus. Letter to Martin. 18 April, 1951. Waterford, CT.

[37] Stevens, "Under the Bridge" *Puppetry Journal* 4.4, 26

[38] Kashosravi, Cambiz, Dir. *Dick Myers: Master Puppeteer*. Perf. Dick Myers, Cambiz, 2004. DVD.

[39] Stevens, Martin. "Under the Bridge" *Puppetry Journal* 17.2, 34

[40] Kashosravi, Cambiz, Dir. *Dick Myers: Master Puppeteer*. Perf. Dick Myers, Cambiz, 2004. DVD.

_____Other Work Cited

Coad, Luman. "The Life of Dick Myers Interview with Luman Coad." Telephone interview. 6 Jan. 2013.

Rose, Rufus. Letter to Martin Stevens. 1 May 1951. Waterford, CT.

Stevens, Martin. Letter to Rufus Rose. 19 Feb. 1951. Middlebury, IN.

___ *Martin Stevens: His Book*. Ed. Luman Coad. N.p." Charlemagne Press, 2002, 101.

___ "Under the Bridge." *Puppetry Journal* 17.2 (1965): 34.

Stevens, Olga. Letter to Rufus & Margo Rose. 6 Mar. 1950. Middlebury, IN

Fig. 10. Housekeeper, cat, and Dick from *Dick Whittington and His Cat*.

In the Limelight

2

1966-1983

Myers' unique style of rod puppetry made its debut on June 25, 1966, at the Puppeteers of America Festival in San Diego, California.[1] At the festival, Myers performed his unique version of *Dick Whittington and His Cat*. The show proved to be a highlight of the festival. Both puppet historian Alan Cook and *Puppetry Journal* editor Paul Eide remembered the show was such a success the festival added additional performances of Myers' show. The story of Dick Whittington was rather fitting for Myers' first successful solo show. *Dick Whittington and His Cat*, by Rufus and Margo Rose, was the first puppet show Myers had seen as a young boy. It is possible Myers' nostalgia for the show influenced his decision to create his own version, though this romantic possibility could also be argued against. At the time, *Dick Whittington and His Cat* was a story that had been over performed by many puppeteers for over a century. Nonetheless, Myers transformed this well-known tale into a unique and inspiring show. As explained by puppeteer William Ludwig:

> We all caught the reflection of it [magic] in Dick Myers' production of *The Story of Dick Whittington and His Cat* – theatrical buoyancy out of technical complexity, a beginning.

21

From *The Story of Dick Whittington*.

Fig. 11. (*Above*) Duck and Dick Whittington.

Fig. 12. (*Top Right*) Dick Whittington poster.

Fig. 13. (*Below Left*) Dick Whittington, Cat, & Alice.

Fig. 14. (*Below*) Farmer & Cat

> Puppetry's magic was somewhere deeply imbedded and layered over within us; the scent of its center held us together.[2]

An additional review by puppeteer Vivian Michael exclaimed:

> The most surprising performance of the San Diego Fest was that of Dick Myers who produced his award-winning production of *Dick Whittington and His Cat.* Dick has been fooling around with this production for (I won't tell how long) but when it finally opened Saturday night of the Fest, it was evident that all the time and labor put into the production had paid off. So great was the applause and approval that Dick was immediately asked to repeat the performance again during the Fest.
>
> *Dick Whittington and His Cat* was simple, direct and from puppets to staging, lighting, voices and music, it had a charm that puppets should have…although there were human characters in the play, their simple designing and studied movement forced them to remain puppets. A sheer delight for everyone who saw it, and no one who saw it Saturday night missed the repeat performance.[3]

These reviews, and many more like them, reveal tremendous public and professional support for this unique show and the soft-spoken man behind the curtain. Not one aspect of the show was singled out. The public appreciated the show in its entirety. In an article for the *Puppetry Journal*, Mollie Falkenstein provided a rich description of the performance of *Dick Whittington and His Cat*:

> The auditorium darkens, then slowly, ever so slowly, a blue 'skyline' lights up the stage, gradually dawning to full daylight to the accompaniment of one of the finest tapes I have yet heard!
>
> Dick Whittington enters, at first Dick appears to move a bit slowly, but then he stops and addresses his remarks DIRECTLY TO YOU! His voice is a wonderful voice, and it IS Dick Whittington. The scene is a country scene, and he meets a farmer who gives him a cat. Dick trudges convincingly uphill

and downdale, and eventually reaches London Town via one of the speediest scene changes ever, and accompanied by that beautiful musical tape. London town has excellent scenery, and is very much enhanced by the entrance stage right of a wonderful character, the housekeeper of the captain who takes Dick under his wing, she has a terrible temper, and her towering rages are always in character and are simply wonderful to behold, especially when she goes flying in and out of the door!

Dick 'washes' an endless pile of dishes under the direction of this same housekeeper, and very much tires of this job, but the accompanying clangs and clatters are enough to keep any audience widely on its toes! (Dick was most kind, and re-played this scene with the curtain pulled back so we could see how he achieved these wonderful effects). His puppets were well thought [out] original version of traditional rod puppets, and operate like clockwork.

After a small ship takes the captain and the cat overseas to find a fortune, they enter the emperor's castle and are entertained by a magician and dancing girls. The cat steals the show, however, by obligingly dealing with the rats. Unlike [in] the old tale, the captain returns the cat to Dick, (because what little boy could bear to part with his furry friend) and so Dick gets both the money AND the cat, with the captain's daughter to boot, although that lies ahead in the wonderful land of make-believe which a quiet man has created from wood and metal, and a little paint here and there. We NEED you, Dick, hang on and make a sequel to *Dick Whittington*.[4]

The performance and story line had not been the only highlights of the show. Respecting Myers' clear and cohesive stylization throughout the performance led Marjorie Batchelder-McPharlin to share admiringly:

This [the stylization in the design of the puppets] has often been accomplished successfully in the design of the heads, but not continued in the design of the rest of the figure such as costume, arms, [and] feet. Dick Myers' puppets for DICK WHITTINGTON are among the few seen recently which are consistent throughout. So are Jim Henson's MUPPETS.[5]

After the success of his performance at the festival, Myers received multiple invitations to perform. In December of 1966, he performed *Dick Whittington and His Cat* at the Detroit Institute of Arts, an important arts center that had supported the work of American puppetry since the 1930s.[6] This venue not only presented Myers' first show, but would also go on to sponsor the debut of his next two shows. In the meantime, the success of *Dick Whittington and His Cat* soon took Myers abroad.

In 1967, Myers was invited to perform *Dick Whittington and His Cat* at the first National Puppetry Festival held in Canada at the University of Waterloo in Ontario. In a review of this festival, Lea Wallace shared:

> The charm that radiates from this well thought-out production is one that typically qualifies the "raison d'etre" for puppetry. This production proves that neither animation, nor movies nor human actors could realize the uniqueness contained in this show [...] If theatre is the synthesis of the arts, PUPPETRY extends the synthesis to the puppet actor. The puppet is a harmonious blend of all the visual elements, created for his life in a particular way. Dick Myers' cartoon-styled extraneous detail was also exemplified in the few but well- contained lines of dialogue and in the use of specific sound effects [...] After the viewing, Dick Myers' *Dick Whittington* remains as fresh as the first viewing.[7]

Myers' *Dick Whittington and His Cat* captured the enthusiastic response of many.

In 1967, Myers was invited to perform *Dick Whittington and His Cat*, at the 1967 Expo (a large world fair) in Montreal, Quebec. The

From ***Cinderella***

Fig. 15. (*Above*) Fred the Mouse & Cinderella from *Cinderella*.

Fig. 16. (*Above*) Dick Myers demonstrating scene from *Cinderella*.

Fig. 17. (*Below Left*) Cinderella & Fairy Godmother

Fig. 18. (*Below*) Myers showing Cinderella at Puppeteers of America National Festival in 1968.

Expo featured many great puppet talents from around the world, including Rufus Rose and German puppeteer Albrect Roser. While at the Expo, Myers met a young puppeteer who was captivated by his work. Her name was Allelu Kurten. Enthralled by Myers' talent, Allelu raved to her husband, John, about this exciting new performer. Once John Kurten watched a later performance, he and Allelu offered Myers a place to stay if he was ever in their area of Hyde Park, New York. At the time, Myers resided in a small cabin in Woodstock, which was not too far from Hyde Park. Later, Myers made his way to Hyde Park to stay briefly with the Kurtens. Myers' "short stay" with the couple turned into a thirteen-year residency. He renamed his puppet company from Puppet Arts of Woodstock, NY to Dick Myers Puppet Arts. Myers moved into the Kurtens' house, bringing with him *Dick Whittington and His Cat*, as well as another production he had been developing since before his premiere at the 1966 festival. The second of Myers' productions was *Cinderella*. Like *Whittington*, the story of *Cinderella* was a very popular tale performed by many puppet theatres. On December 16, 1967, Myers' *Cinderella* made its debut at the Detroit Puppet Theatre located in the Detroit Institute of Arts.[8] Following this performance, in April of 1968, Myers performed *Cinderella* for the Department of Massachusetts Marine Corps.[9] Although these two performances of *Cinderella* were significant, the show did not receive much acknowledgement at first. However, this all changed on August 20, 1968, when Myers performed at the 1968 National Puppetry Festival in St. Louis, Missouri. The reviews for Myers' *Cinderella* proved it was even more successful than the performances of *Dick Whittington and His Cat*. Puppeteer Joe Ayers stated in a 1968 festival review:

> "An Evening with Dick Myers." His unforgettable *Dick Whittington* had been supplemented with an even-better *Cinderella* to provide a full program. For you poor, benighted people who have never seen Dick Myers' work I will TRY to describe the experience. Dick uses rod-puppets made entirely of plastic wood. They are extremely stylized, so they almost resemble well-drawn cartoons.

> The settings are also stylized, and as he works without a curtain the settings assemble themselves between scenes in an intriguing manner. Dick's scripts manage to invest these overworked stories with a new, tongue-in-cheek quality that entrances adults as well as children. For example, in *Cinderella* there is no flashpot as the transformations are accomplished: Fairy Godmother: 'You need a new dress...You know the rules, go outside'...Cinderella exits, and appears a moment later in her dress for the ball! Evidently the audience was in agreement that Dick Myers is something special, for he got standing ovations for both *Dick Whittington* and *Cinderella*![10]

At this point in Myers' career, his two successful shows were taking him all over North America, including Canada. In 1968, his performance boundaries expanded when he received an invitation to perform at an International Puppetry Festival in Colwyn Bay, Wales. At this festival, Myers performed both *Dick Whittington and His Cat* and *Cinderella*. Betsy Brown noted, "Dick Myers not only represented [the United States of America] with distinction, but elevated the whole world of puppetry".[11] Additionally, Kenneth N. Crawford wrote of the highly respectable work of Myers:

> Dick Myers was a new name to Britain and he astonished many people with his one man show with rod puppets which moved in a very similar manner to marionettes. His audiences were delighted with truly English pantomimes, *Cinderella* and *Dick Whittington*. Well-modeled, stylized figures made of plastic wood, with 'walking' legs, moveable heads and arms, all lever controlled from below, they all adopted most acceptable poses when standing 'dead' on stage. Most interesting vaudeville turns were skillfully inserted in the programme, which greatly added to the fun in the show. Unlikely turns were a trampoline act and a mechanical organ. Excellent lighting, colour, music and scenery made this a charming show.[12]

Many more puppeteers spoke of the unique and fresh work that Myers had to offer, including German puppeteer, Bühne Friedrich

Arndt. In a letter he wrote to Myers, he expressed how much he enjoyed his performance in Calwyn Bay, Wales:

> Dick Myers does not imitate live theatre with his puppets but his form of playing entirely corresponds to the nature of puppets. This becomes obvious already by the stylized figures which forego any naturalism with so much success. These puppets excel by the simplified and concentrated expression of their faces and features, caricating [sic] human characters without losing their amiability even for a single moment. [...] During the performance, pictures which could well be excellent illustrations for fairy tales appear again and again, thus making the whole an aesthetic delight. [...] What he offered was genuine artistic puppet theatre of top of quality, a charming but at the same time clear image of our human world.[13]

In April of 1969, Myers made his first and only American televised appearance. "Dick Myers video-taped a special all-puppet show for Boston's [children television show] *Bozo Show*. He condensed his show, *Cinderella*, to fit in a half-hour program shown in April".[14] Puppeteer Caroll Spinney, who had been working with Boston's *Bozo Show* at that time, confirms this television event, though he doubts there are any recorded copies of the performance still in existence. He explains, "they just didn't know what they had." It is possible the studio may have recorded over the show, because new videotape was at the time quite expensive. With a television performance to add to his list of experiences, Myers continued performing his two shows throughout America.

While performing *Cinderella* and *Dick Whittington and His Cat*, Myers was building and perfecting a third upcoming one-man show, *Beauty and the Beast*. Once again, Myers chose a story that was immensely popular within the field of puppetry performance. To a greater extent than many other puppet versions of this story, Myers' adaptation of the tale was unique and quirky. *Beauty and the Beast* premiered in mid-November of 1969 at the Detroit Institute of Arts. Myers performed to full houses. At this point

From ***Cinderella***.

Fig. 19. (*Top*) Fairy Godmother, Fred (as a horse) and Cinderella.

Fig. 20. (*Middle*) Organ Grinder at Prince's Ball.

Fig. 21 (*Bottom*) Finding Cinderella's Shoe.

in his career, Myers felt confident and secure. As described by Don Avery, "Dick says that he has one more major production to complete, then he'll be satisfied to sit back and look for ways he can do the whole thing better."[15] Following his performance at the Detroit Institute of Arts, Myers performed *Beauty and the Beast* as part of a final show in a five-part children's theatre series. This performance took place at Chicago's Beverly Art Center. Nearly a year after Myers premiered his newest show for family audiences, he finally performed it for his peers. On August 18, 1970, the professional puppetry community finally had the opportunity to watch Myers' *Beauty and the Beast*. This performance took place at the 1970 National Puppetry Festival held at the University of Connecticut in Storrs, Connecticut. After the performance, Joe Ayers wrote:

> Dick Myers' *Beauty and the Beast* brought a tumultuous applause...and a standing ovation to this national celebrity. [...] I must pass out orchids to Dick Myers' [...] 'superstar' Dick had a four-column interview in the New York Times![16]

Similarly, puppeteer, Basil Milovsoroff, shared:

> In 1953 (July) I wrote an article for *Theatre Arts* magazine entitled 'Reality with Strings Attached" (a title suggested by Bil Baird) in which I restated the three cardinal elements in Puppet Theatre production which have emerged from a number of minds concerned with the whys and wherefores of the Puppet Theatre, namely, *abstraction, motion,* and *synthesis*. Richard, it appears, has come ideally close to achieving these in his charming, sophisticated interpretation of the old familiar tale *Beauty and the Beast.* The competent simplicity of design and lighting, verbal economy with superb use of the pause, and honest motion inherent and permitted by the mechanics of the design have given the performance not only the style of unmistakable individuality, authority and perfection, but offered credibility as *Theatre,* meaning in the simplest terms, unreserved enjoyment of a performance. It was a gentle

From ***Beauty and the Beast***.

Fig. 22. (*Above*) Richard the Mouse, the Potion Machine, and the Witch.

Fig.23. (*Top Right*) Myers with the Raulo's (the Beast) parents at the dining table.

Fig. 24. (*Right*) Beast and Geraldine.

> comedy devoid of either speech or action vulgarisms which so often destroy our attempts to make Theatre with puppets, a comedy which by its unexpected humorous sequel ever so unobtrusively touched upon a profound moral. The longest standing ovation that I have ever witnessed at a puppet performance was so rightfully deserved. Bravo, Dick Myers! Encore! Encore! Encore![17]

After the successful performance at the festival, Myers sought out any opportunity he could to perform his puppetry, even if it was unplanned.

In 1971, Myers brought *Cinderella* to the National Puppetry Festival in Nashville, Tennessee. The performance of this show was unscheduled, but turned out to be one of the most successful shows at the festival.[18] Additionally, he offered an extensive workshop. Myers discussed information about many of his techniques including puppet building, lighting, sound, and his technique for creating pop-up sets out of cardboard, glue, and muslin. Admiration for Myers' hard work and dedication in the field of puppetry spread internationally.

In 1972, Myers received a prestigious invitation to perform at the International UNIMA Festival in Charleville-Mezieres, France. In an article in the 1972 *Puppetry Journal*, Marie Saminksy shared:

> Dick Myers left our shores in August for a year to travel and to perform throughout Europe. He was at the Syon Park Puppet Festival, Middlesex, England in August, and at the Little Angel Theatre in London early in September. He represented the United States giving five performances at the UNIMA Fest[ival] in [Charleville-Mezieres] France, and during October he toured Sweden, Denmark, and Norway. He expects to remain in Europe through the summer of 1973.[19]

While in Europe, Myers also toured Germany and Switzerland.[20] The work of Dick Myers proved to be universally appreciated.

From **Simple Simon**.

Fig. 25. (*Top*) King, Baby William, Juggler, & Pierrot.

Fig. 26. (*Middle*) At the fair.

Fig. 27. (*Right*) Simon's Parents

Allelu Kurten offered a summary that explained why Myers' work was universal and adored by countries abroad:

> Dick Myers who, with the minimum of dialogue, with extreme care in piecing of high quality tapes, development of ingenious puppets and the removal of every non-essential, produces a simple, direct, and perfect theatrical effect. There is tremendous thought before anything is done.[21]

Freshly returned from abroad, Myers received yet another invitation to perform at a puppetry festival, the 1973 Puppeteers of America Festival in Lansing, Michigan. Myers performed his successful and delightful *Beauty and the Beast.* Once again, his puppetry received respectable acknowledgement. Nancy B. Henk noted:

> Dick Myers is a perfectionist when it comes to choosing music for his puppet productions and it seems to me that his selections always represent just the right mood and scale. His choice of music for the divertissement which appear in most of his productions never fails to delight me with its variety. (...and now, Baby William will play for you!)[22]

Satisfied with the three shows he had created, Myers began putting together a fourth show.

The fourth of Myers' unique rod-puppet shows was labored over for years (Fig. 25). As early as 1972, Myers mentioned working on one final show and then dedicating his career to perfecting all four productions. The fourth show he had been working on was an hour-long production derived from the short English nursery rhyme, *Simple Simon*. The content of the nursery rhyme is as follows:

> Simple Simon met a pieman,
> Going to the fair;
> Says Simple Simon to the pieman,
> Let me taste your ware.
> Says the pieman to Simple Simon,

From **Simple Simon**.

Fig 28. (*Above*) Simon and Mariamne's Balancing Act from *Simple Simon*.

Fig. 29. (*Above Right*) Baby William, xylophone virtuoso from *Beauty and the Beast*.

Fig. 30. (*Right*) Juggler from *Beauty and the Beast*.

> Show me first your penny;
> Says Simple Simon to the pieman,
> Indeed I have not any.

Myers premiered *Simple Simon* at the 1975 National Puppetry Festival in St. Charles, Missouri. Although this production was charming and perfect in design and performance, it did not receive as much acclaim as his other productions. In a review of the 1975 festival, David Sears wrote:

> For me, the work was still in preparation, not ready for criticism. Suffice it to say, Mr. Myers has developed the one-person puppet show in a most amazing way, creating intricate spring mechanisms within his rod puppets, a technique undoubtedly related to his many years' work as [an] airplane pilot and mechanic. In this production, Mr. Myers presented more than enough circus skits to delight his audience, a virtuoso display of his newest inventions and off-handed wit. Clumsy Simon learned to balance both a chicken and his girlfriend on the end of a stick, so entertaining the king cum [*sic*] pieman that he was elevated to the post of Royal Prime Minister. In contrast to this skyscraper feat, Mr. Myers was equally content to present a puppet with absolutely no controls – a dance of gravitational whimsy. This effect reinforced the freedom of the presentation, at once as precise yet comfortable as a Swiss clock. Where the production faded, however, was in the emphasis of skits over plot development. The audience's attention quickly focused on the mechanics rather than the story. If, as he has said, he wanted to mask the fact that he is a one-person show, this balance needed reworking. Mr. Myers is indeed a glorious gymnast, and the production made this obvious.[23]

Although *Simple Simon* did not herald the same respect as his previous shows, it still proved successful enough to go abroad.

In 1976, Myers was the only American invited to perform at the Twelfth Congress of UNIMA, which took place in Moscow,

USSR.[24] With this invitation, Myers once again took the opportunity to tour Europe, (much like in 1972-1973). He traveled to Great Britain, France, Germany, Denmark, Sweden, Poland, the USSR, and the Faroe Islands.[25] He offered *Simple Simon* for this tour. While in Europe, Myers' work was so well received that he was awarded a medal for his excellence in puppetry. This medal was bestowed upon him by one of the greatest world puppet performers of the time, Sergi Obraztzov.[26] After this bestowment, Myers traveled to Catalonia, Spain, where he performed at the International Puppet Festival. Don Avery wrote about the performance:

> Dick Myers' *Simple Simon* [...] was the only American contribution to the Festival. At the end of the show, Myers did a number in view of the audience, demonstrating the complexities of his one-man operation of music, lights, and intricately contrived rod puppets. To the critic Joan Castells, Myers seemed, during this part of his program, 'like a fish in the water'.[27]

Since the beginning of his solo career, Myers would drop the curtain of his puppet booth after his show, revealing the complexity of his apparently simple shows. Puppeteer Allelu Kurten remembered the delight in Myers' spirit when he made this post-show reveal, "Dick became another person after he performed. It is as if it gave him special life. He had communicated what he really wanted to communicate to an audience."[28]

After returning from Europe, Myers had hope his tour schedule in America would quickly fill. He was not a great self publicist, and rarely sought out gigs on his own. Instead Myers hoped word-of-mouth would be enough to book his calendar with shows. This was, unfortunately, not the case. Myers continued to perform his shows at festivals, but festivals did not bring a substantial income.

Nevertheless, in the summer of 1977, Myers received the opportunity to perform at the Puppeteers of America Festival in San Luis Obispo, California. For this festival show, he performed *Cinderella*. Yet again, the show was an enormous success. In a review of the show, Michael R. Malkin stated, "Dick Myers operates on his own and totally original wave length […] [His] odd world of puppetry is a unique and special place that is well worth visiting and revisiting. He is a puppeteer's puppeteer".²⁹ Richard Termine shared similar sentiments:

> Dick Myers' *Cinderella* achieves the ultimate in puppet stylization; simplicity […] The mechanical rod puppets used, meet the needs of his solo performance. Yet, Mr. Myers' superb manipulation contradicts the physical limitations of these stiff puppets. Their variety and articulation of expression is a lesson in itself. Correspondingly, the dialogue captures their vocal image, as the sound and sparcity of language helps the puppets come alive in a world totally their own. […] The uniqueness and integration of this production belongs to the singularness of its creator, Dick Myers. His individual approach distinguishes his work, making it an art.³⁰

Dick Whittington and His Cat, Cinderella, Beauty and the Beast, and even *Simple Simon* had each captured the hearts of audiences. The charm, wittiness, and subtle complexity of his shows had made him a success among his peers. Myers decided to develop a new show.

In creating his new show, Myers was determined to break away from his classic, charming routine. He decided to create an experimental production geared towards adult audiences. In the early stages of its development, Myers referred to the show as his *Experimental Puppetry* program, but later, he changed the show's title to *Divertisement*. It was comprised of two one-hour parts. Each part included vignettes (singular stories with no direct correlation to each other) that ranged from the humorous to the mournful, and from visually stimulating to bizarre. As in every Myers show, the character of Baby William was featured playing various musical instruments. In *Divertisement*, Baby William played the bass drum, violin, accordion, harmonica, xylophone, and trombone. Unlike previous shows, *Divertisement* was comprised entirely of music.

From **Cinderella**.

Fig. 31. (*Above*) Short Step-sister's disapproval.

Fig. 32. (*Right*) Short and Tall Step-sisters.

Fig. 32. Guital Player from *Beauty and the Beast*.:

With songs by composers such as classical Mozart and experimental John Cage, the music in this show could best be described as eclectic.

At the Puppeteers of America 39th National Puppetry Festival in Lubbock, Texas, Myers once again presented an unforgettable departure, but this time, he did not receive the same response. His initial performance of *Beauty and the Beast* went well as usual; naturally, the audience loved Myers' performance. As described in the 1978 *Puppetry Journal*, "As always, the audience reacts admiringly to a charming approach in a style that is clearly Dick Myers"[31]. But his new show, *Divertisement,* did not receive the usual rave response. In fact, there was not one review of this performance. The audience found the show to be slow moving and without Myers' usual charm. Discouraged, Myers felt American puppeteers were not ready to accept the next generation of his work. *Divertisement* was a show that was decades before its time. Today this show might be well received, as it seems congruent to the current post-modernism drama movements that are happening around the world.

By 1978, Myers had grown frustrated with American puppetry, and set out to create a new entity. He started by reinventing his own image. Instead of calling himself Dick Myers, he now presented his work under the puppeteer name, Milo Myers. Additionally, he changed the name of his puppet theatre. Originally known as the Dick Myers Puppet Arts (and also called Dick Myers Puppet Theatre at times) it was changed to The Mad Butterfly Puppet Theatre of Milo Myers. This new theatre name was put on later advertisements for *Divertisement*. Still, however, Myers' new show was only presented at a few public performances.

Realizing *Divertisement* would not be the success for which he had hoped, he returned to his traditional performance roots. Myers put together what became known as a college/concert series. The first part of the program was a performance of one of Myers' four fairytale shows: *Dick Whittington and His Cat, Cinderella, Beauty and*

the Beast, and *Simple Simon*. The second half of the show was dedicated to his experimental vignettes. Even with the addition of his classic shows, Myers' new work went unrecognized. Soon after, he left his experimental work behind and returned wholly to the classic work for which he was known.

In 1978, UNIMA offered Myers an opportunity to tour Japan with his beloved classic show, *Cinderella*. This thirty-two-day tour ran from November 13 through December 15. Although Myers always worked alone, UNIMA insisted he bring with him an assistant. UNIMA chose Nancy Laverick to serve as Myers' tour assistant and photographer. Before the tour, Myers rehearsed *Cinderella* in his puppet studio (which was still generously rent free on the grounds of the Kurtens' residence). Of course, he found little need for an assistant, and also did not like the idea of anyone else handling his puppets. Therefore, Laverick spent much of her time conversing with the Kurtens during Myers' rehearsal time. As a sendoff for Myers' Japan tour, Laverick arranged for Myers to perform at the Puppet Show Place Theatre in Brookline, Massachusetts. This performance was well received and served as an example of what the tour abroad would be like. Laverick described the success of Myers' shows in Japan:

> Opening night brought a full house to the Puk Theatre which holds 125 people. The show went off beautifully and was very well received. Dick was presented with flowers at the curtain call (a custom he was adjusted to by the time the tour ended). He took down the front curtain and with the help of Noda-san explained how the puppets worked while I took pictures through the stage. The audience asked all kinds of questions which Noda-san translated to Dick and then translated his answers into Japanese. It was a very interesting ritual and became a part of the 'act' since many of the same questions were repeated after each performance during the five weeks and Noda-san, our interpreter, had to pretend she didn't know the answers.[32]

Myers' work had transcended international borders yet again. His simple yet complex charming shows had proven to set a strong respectable presence throughout the world.

In 1980, Myers received an invitation to perform at the International Puppetry Festival in Washington, D.C., but frustrated with American puppeteers, Myers decided to decline the invitation and thus missed one of the most significant international puppetry festivals of the 20th century, where Jim Henson filmed all the performances and interviewed the artists. Instead Myers booked a tour across Great Britain, but due to poor planning, this tour abroad proved to be a financial disaster. Without any earnings, Myers could not even afford to ship his puppets and theatre back to the United States. He had no choice but to store his show in the garage of British puppeteer, Penny Francis. He also had to sell his tour van (an old Chevrolet painted school-bus yellow with padlocks on every door and wires spread across its body, giving the appearance of an alarm system) in order to purchase a ticket back to the United States.

Once he returned to the United States, Myers moved out of the Kurtens' residence and returned to his childhood home in Elkhart, Indiana, where he stayed with his sister, Marietta. Hearing of Myers' disaster abroad, John and Allelu Kurten arranged a fundraiser dinner at their home to help him. Everyone invited to the dinner had at one point or another allowed Myers to stay at their home; there were enough people to fill two banquet tables. By the end of the dinner, the guests and the Kurtens had put together enough money to have Myers' puppets shipped from England to the US. Although the puppets were returned to him, Myers was still not able to perform a show. Without a vehicle, he could no longer share his puppetry as he once had. Once more, Myers had to try to start again.

In 1983, Myers moved to Toronto, Ontario, with hope for a fresh beginning. Specifically, he hoped to acquire Canadian residency and to reestablish his puppet theatre, but regrettably, neither of

these hopes would come to be. He was offered a rent-free apartment owned by puppeteer, Johan Vandergun, but in 1983, Myers received only one booking. This performance took place at the Discovery Theatre located at the Smithsonian in Washington D.C. Myers performed his classic show, *Cinderella*, from Wednesday May 4 through Sunday, June 5. These performances were the last of his career. Not long afterwards, the Discovery Theatre began to film and archive every performance held there. Once again, Myers missed an opportunity to have his shows documented. After six months in Canada, Myers returned to the place he had always called home: Elkhart, Indiana.

---

[1] Michael, Vivian, ed. "1966 Festival, San Diego, California." *Puppetry Journal* 17.4 (1966): 28.

[2] Ludwig, G. William. "Personal Impressions of a First Festival." *Puppetry Journal* 18.1 (1966):6.

[3] Michaels, Vivian, ed. "Puppet Parade." *Puppetry Journal* 18.2 (1966): 12.

[4] Falkenstein, Mollie. "Dick Whittington." *Puppetry Journal* 18.3 1966): 30.

[5] Batchelder-McPharlin, Marjorie. "Puppets in Action." *Puppetry Journal* 18.5 (1967): 7.

[6] Stevens, Martin. "Under the Bridge." *Puppetry Journal* 18.4 (1967): 41.

[7] Wallace, Lea. "Dick Whittington." *Puppetry* Journal 19.1 (1967): 16.

[8] Stevens, Martin. "Under the Bridge" *Puppetry Journal* 19.4 (1968): 24.

[9] Young, Rod. "Substituting for Steve." *Puppetry Journal* 19.6 (1968): 27.

[10] Ayers, Joe. "Tuesday August 20th." *Puppetry Journal* 20.2 (1968): 9.

[11] Brown, Betsy. "One Man Show at Colwyn Bay." *Puppetry Journal* 20.2 (1968): 34.

[12] Crawford, Kenneth H. "Colwyn Bay Festival." *Puppetry Journal* 20.3 (1968): 25-29.

[3] Arndt, Bühne F. Letter to Dick Myers. 10 Sept. 1968.

[14] Smith, Larry. "Behind the Scenes." *Puppetry Journal* 20.6 (1969): 38-40.

[15] Avery, Don, ed. "Puppet Picture Section." *Puppetry Journal* 21.3 (1969): 18.

[16] Ayers, Joe. "Festival 70, an Overview." *Puppetry Journal* 22 (1970): 26-27.

[17] Milovsoroff, Basil. "Towards a Better Puppet Theatre" *Puppetry Journal* 22.4 (1971): 7-8.

[18] Milovsoroff Basil. "Impression, Impressions, Impressions of Festival '71." 23.2 (1971): 15.

[19] Samanisky, Marie. "The Spotlight" *Puppetry Journal* 24.3 (1972): 36.

[20] Samanisky, Marie. "The Spotlight" *Puppetry Journal* 24.6, (1973): 27.

[21] Kurten, Allelu. "Contact with our Consultants." *Puppetry Journal* 24.6 (1973): 33.

[22] Henk, Nancy. "The Magic of Music." *Puppetry Journal* 26.1 (1974): 62-65.

[23] Sears, David. "National Puppetry Festival Review." *Puppetry Journal* 27.1 (1975): 28-39.

[24] Lords, Daniel. "International Notebook." *Puppetry Journal* 27.4. (1976): 40.

[25] Salter, Ted. "Caricature of the Month, Dick Myers." *Puppetry Journal* 29-3 (1977): 38.

[26] Salter, Ted. "Caricature of the Month, Dick Myers." *Puppetry Journal* 29-3 (1977): 38.

[27] Avery, Don. "With Pride We Report" *Puppetry Journal* 28.4 (1977): 40.

[28] Kurten, Allelu. "The Life of Dick Myers." Personal Interview. 6 Dec. 2012.

[29] Malkin, Michael R. "Puppeteers of America 38th National Festival in Review." *Puppetry Journal* 29.2 (1977): 19.

[30] Termine, Richard. "Performance Review." *Puppetry Journal* 29.2 (1977): 24.

[31] Avery, Don "Festival Diary" *Puppetry Journal* 30.1 (1978): 22

[32] Laverick, Nancy. "Dick Myers' Cinderella Tours Japan" *Puppetry Journal* 30.6 (1979): 16.

3

Retirement

1983-2005

By late 1983, Myers returned to Indiana where he decided to remove himself entirely from the world of puppetry. Using his middle name, Dick Myers would now be known as Milo Myers. Limited information can be found about Myers' life during this time, except he would ride a bike everywhere he went, and he remained active in society. In 1986, Myers was a participant in The Great Peace March for Nuclear Disarmament. In a letter to the Kurtens, Myers wrote, "On The Great Peace March, every couple of weeks we had 'Hug-A-Day.' Imagine 800 people out in a field, all hugging each other."[1]

In 1993, Myers attempted unsuccessfully to revive his work for the Puppeteers of America Festival in San Francisco, California. Spending many hours a day rehearsing, the 71-year-old puppeteer found it difficult to build up the strength and endurance he had once possessed for his shows. Though performing at this festival was not possible, he continued to re-explore his puppetry and different ideas for shows. He began working on a variety show titled, *The Baby William Show*. This show would feature all the musical acts of Baby William, but the title was never announced (or performed) and can be found only as a title marked into one of Myers' puppet boxes.

Fig. 33. UNIMA Citations were awarded to three of Dick Myers' productions:

Beauty and the Beast,

Cinderella, and

Simple Simon.

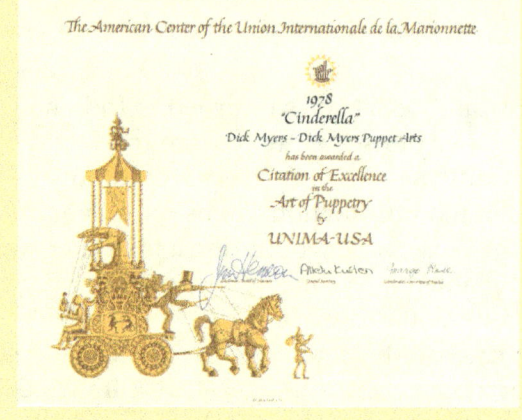

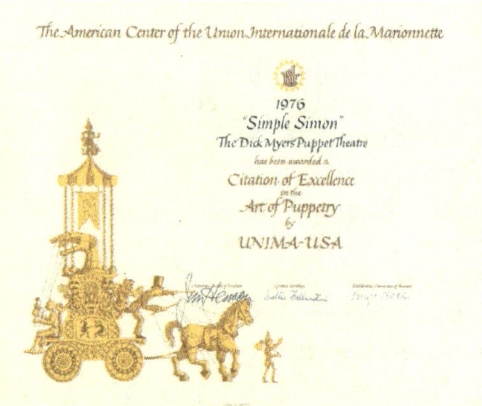

Besides *The Baby William Show*, Myers also began working on a twenty-minute piece called, *The Mall Show*, featuring his circus style acts from *Simple Simon*. There is an existing audiotape for this show, indicating Myers intended to mount this production. However, he knew he could not do the show alone. In a letter to the Kurtens, Myers wrote:

> In Jan[uary] of this year (while working with 'Cinderella') I collapsed – crawled to [the] phone-dialed 911 and passed out. 'Came to' in the hospital with a 'pace maker' in my chest. All's well now – all's returning to normal [...] I can't 'handle' my shows solo [...] I thought-Whoa! Give them to somebody who cares – give 'The Dick Myers Puppet Theatre' to them...Then I thought, whoa! Yes, give them everything, but just because one person can't handle a show, doesn't mean that the three of us couldn't do a great show.[2]

Despite Myers' enthusiasm, he was unable to follow through with this proposal. Slowly, he seemed to acknowledge the fact that age had caught up with him and the shows were too costly to revive.

In 1999, Myers received a letter from Paul Mesner, which offered hope of finding assistance remounting his shows. In the letter Mesner shared:

> I have been an enthusiastic fan of yours since I first attended one of your shows at a puppet festival. I was fourteen at the time and was profoundly impressed with your ability to perform a wonderfully funny show as a sole puppeteer. [...] I feel very strongly that your shows should not end up in some forgotten storage. Therefore, I would like to discuss with you the potential of a cooperative effort in preserving your exceptional talent. I wish to see your artistry preserved so that many generations to come may enjoy the loving humor I experienced 28 years ago.[3]

Myers moved out to Kansas City to accept this opportunity, but it soon became clear his requests were too costly. In a letter to the Kurtens, Myers wrote, "it was too expensive to provide 'board and room' for me [...] I went back to Elkhart [...] not to return to Kansas City".[4]

Fig. 34. Myers with friend Nancy Angeloch.

Fig. 35. Myers rehearsing *Simple Simon* at home.

Once Myers returned to Elkhart, he discovered the house he was living in had been sold. Years earlier, his sister Marietta had passed away, leaving the house to her son. With the inability to perform and now the loss of his childhood home, Myers turned to his resources. Soon after, he would move into a hotel in town. Seeking out his second family, Myers wrote letters to many of his close friends: Jane Henson, Bart Roccoberton Jr., and the Kurtens. Shortly after, his dear friend and talented artist, Nancy Angeloch, opened her home to Myers and his entire puppet collection, and encouraged him to once again try to revive his life's work.

In his final years, Myers worked hard to revive his shows, but in the end, he was physically unable to perform any of his shows. With the hope of preserving Myers' work, friends Angeloch and Susan Weeks arranged a videographer to film an interview with Myers. Cambiz A. Khosravi arrived at Angeloch's home and filmed Myers attempting to rehearse *Cinderella* and documented Myers talking about his life and career as a puppeteer. Afterwards, Khosravi condensed many hours of footage into a twenty-one-minute documentary, titled, *Dick Myers: Master Puppeteer*. Despite his inability to perform, Myers did not want to give up on seeing his shows performed again, so he placed an ad in a paper for an apprentice puppeteer. But he didn't find anyone suitable, as he wrote to the Kurtens, "this did not work out".[5]

In 2004, Angeloch was diagnosed with Alzheimer's disease and wished to live alone,[6] so Myers found residence at the Saugerties Senior Home. He found this housing to be rather intolerable. In a letter to Allelu, Myers wrote, "It is quite like a morgue, all that folks talk about is food – no art, no music, no theatre, no puppets".[7] Soon after, Myers developed vertigo, which made it impossible once and for all to remount his work. On April 28, 2005, 83-year-old Myers passed away at Kingston Hospital. In remembrance of Myers, Allelu Kurten wrote:

> How Dick managed to have as many as 6 of his puppets on stage at one time – dancing, playing instruments and, on occasion, sticking out their tongues – is still a wonder to his fans. His rocket science and technical skills enabled him to construct a

Fig. 36. Myers in his apartment at Saugerties Senior Housing. Saugerties. NY.

Fig. 37. Lunch after a bike ride.

complex series of controls within each rod and a complicated orchestration of sound and action backstage while, from the front, quiet brilliance made it SO simple. He was a solo 'CLASS ACT'![8]

The world of puppetry lost one of the most talented and unique puppeteers it had ever seen. Myers' puppets would now lie in their boxes, waiting to be performed again.

Myers' entire puppetry collection had been left at the houses of his dear friends, Nancy Angeloch and Susan Weeks. They both desired to have Myers' final wish fulfilled, for his shows to be remounted. Angeloch offered the puppets to Allelu Kurten, who immediately offered the project to Bart Roccoberton, the director of the University of Connecticut's Puppet Arts Program. Roccoberton obtained the puppets and stored them away with every intention of having the shows one day remounted and documented. In the 2006 *Puppetry Journal,* Alleu Kurten wrote:

> He [Roccoberton] was eager to bring [the puppets] to UCONN and offer them a new life. He plans to catalogue the collection and, hopefully, obtain a grant to enable students to mount and perform some parts if not all of one or two of the shows (at least 'Cinderella' and 'Beauty and the Beast'). Dick kept very clear, verbally annotated rehearsal tapes which we hope can be 'revitalized' along with the performance tapes. And here we hold our breath.[9]

The remounting of his work seemed an impossible task. *Woodstock Times* author Sigrid Heath wrote:

> It is nearly impossible [...] to imagine anyone other than Dick Myers doing his shows. His heart behind the characters gives them life. Another performer might bring other qualities, but it seems clear that what's vital, what's *true* about Cinderella's friend Fred, for example, is Myers.[10] (Fig. C.5)

Dick Myers will forever be known as one of the great puppeteers of the 20th century. As expressed by Frank Oz (performer of Ms.

Piggy, Yoda, and Fozzie Bear to name a few), "I consider Dick Myers to be one of the most original puppeteers working in the world today. His performances and his puppets are a delight."[11]

---

[1] Myers, Dick. Letter to the Kurtens N.d.

[2] Myers, Dick. Letter to the Kurtens. May 22

[3] Mesner, Paul. Letter to Dick Myers. June 29, 1999

[4] Myers, Dick. Letter to Allelu and John Kurten Oct 20, 1999

[5] Myers, Dick. Letter to Allelu and John Kurten no date

[6] Myers, Dick. Letter to Allelu, June 2004

[7] Myers, Dick. Letter to Allelu, not dated.

[8] Kurten, Allelu. "Dick Myers," Puppetry Journal 56.4 (2006): 31.)

[9] Kurten, Allelu. "Saving Dick Myers Puppetry for Posterity." *Puppetry Journal* 58-1 (2006): 8.

[10] Heath, Sigrid. "Master Puppet Dick Myers is Ready to Settle Down." *Woodstick Times* Nov. 2003: 1+.

[11] Oz, Frank. Letter of Recommendation to Dick Myers. nd.

4

Myers Mechanisms

Dick Myers' puppets and puppet booth were an engineering marvel. He placed thought and precision into every element of each puppet, no matter how short it was on stage during the show. Many of his puppets had similar control mechanisms. However some puppets had unique movements or shapes which prohibited the "traditional" Myers' mechanisms. In these cases, he spent a lot of time precisely engineering a mechanism to give the puppet the desired movement.

In this chapter, I will attempt to comprehensively illustrate Myers' mechanisms and technical aspects of his stage. Throughout the coming chapter, I will break down how the puppets operate as well as how the puppet booth design eases the puppeteer's ability to perform a one-person show.

Through my research, I discovered Myers' puppet booth underwent several transformations. While the article he had wrote in the *Puppetry Journal* outlined a hand puppet booth (quite different from his rod puppet booth), his actual hand puppet booth was the first rendition of what would later be his booth (only shorter, with a half-circle cyclorama instead of a rectangular one). Myers' puppet booth had many secrets to share, and later in the book I will go into detail about how it fit together.

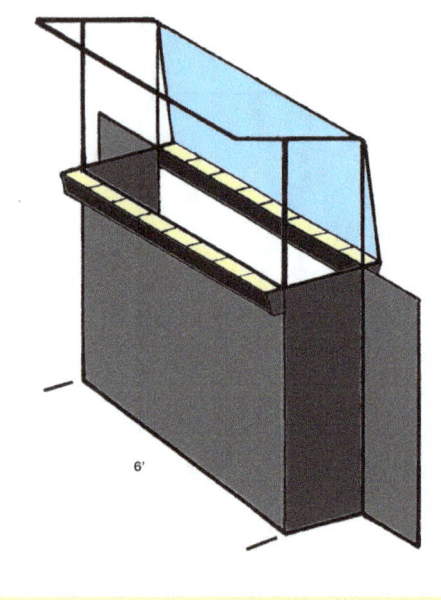

Fig. 38. (*Above*) Simplified drawing of Myers' rod puppet stage.

Fig. 39. (*Top Right*) Seth in front of Myers' rod puppet stage.

Fig. 40. (*Middle Right*) Slotted Shelf

Fig. 41. (*Bottom Right*) Carving craters in slotted shelf.

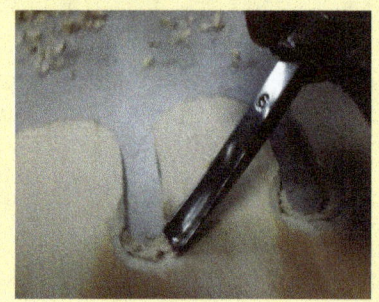

Myers' rod puppet booth measures 6' wide by 2' deep and it's playboard is 6'4" off the ground. At the far upstage part of the booth is a 1" x 2" piece of wood which runs all the way across the 6' stage. This is the scenery bar, which is where the set pieces clip onto the stage. Behind this is a bright blue cyclorama lit by a long row of 40-watt clear appliance bulbs covered with a blue lighting gel. The cyclorama extends the 6' length of the stage and is approximately 2'8" tall (making the stage 8'5" from the ground to the top of the cyclorama). All the way downstage and below the play-board, are a set of 40-watt clear tube light bulbs (directly wrapped in blue and orange lighting gels) which shine up onto the puppets as footlights.

The main lighting bar is 9'6" above the ground. The lighting bar is supported by a 1" x 2" on each end, branching off the main cyclorama support. The light bar's height is set by two metal rods with hooks (one on each end) that can be lowered to 8'6" if needed (the same height as the cyclorama). There are eight lights on the lighting bar. Three of these lights have 300-watt flood lights inside (with orange and blue gels), while the other five are hand-made instruments with 100-watt bulb lights (with blue gels).

The puppet booth has 20" wings to mask the backstage on both sides. The stage right side wing hides the lighting box which controls each section of lights individually (except the cyclorama, which is on a separate switch located just above the lighting box).

Most of Myers' puppets remain at the playboard height because of the special slotted shelf system he developed. The slots run the nearly entire 6' length of the puppet booth and are approximately 8" below the playboard (there is a small open space center stage to give more space to specialty puppet operations). Most of the puppets have two disks which sandwich around the shelf through the slot system. When a puppet is in this position, its feet are directly at the playboard level.

Fig. 40 shows an example of the slotted shelves. There are two slotted shelves just like this, which bolt directly onto the puppet booth. The openings in this shelf are approximately 1½" apart and the slots are approximately ½" wide and 3" deep. The Masonite circles are examples of the disks that are attached to the puppets.

Fig. 42 & 43. Operating the Myers' rod puppets.

At the inner most part of the slots, Myers carved away a circular crater to allow the puppets to hang upside-down on the playboard for easy access during a scene. (Fig. 41) Most of Myers' puppets have a 1⅛" Plastic Wood ball on the bottom which sits perfectly into this crater while the puppet is suspended upside-down on the playboard. This ensures the puppet will not slide off the slotted shelf unit if it is accidentally bumped.

On the right and left side of the stage, there are shorter slotted shelf systems. These are used to hold and organize the puppets during the show. The shorter slotted shelves are approximately two feet long and located approximately 3½' from the ground. The smaller slotted shelves are not removable, instead they are hinged on the puppet booth and can fold up into the booth during the tear down of the puppet booth. These extra slotted shelves are essential for quick and easy access to the puppets during the one-person shows. Additional props and puppets are stored on the puppet booth with hook eyes and clips. During a show, everything has a place and it is essential each puppet, prop, and set piece is preset in the appointed place backstage.

Understanding the basics of Myers' mechanisms is essential in understanding how his puppets move. Figure 43 is a diagram of the control handle Myers used for many of his puppets. The measurements are mostly consistent from puppet to puppet, however there are some slight differences depending on the puppet.

The control handle offers different "buttons" and levers to manage the actions of each puppet. Some puppets have specific actions and movements which Myers' workshopped and adapted to the puppets to achieve his desired movements. I had heard Myers would sometimes be frustrated in the amount of time it would take to figure out how to construct a mechanism to achieve the movement precisely as he wished. When it comes to creating these mechanisms, precision is key. There is almost no room for error; one bad joint could make the mechanisms bind up and not work smoothly.

The control handles of Myers' puppets are made with a 1" dowel. This dowel has a ⅜" hole drilled from the top to the area where the mechanism rods come out of the handle. Once this hole was

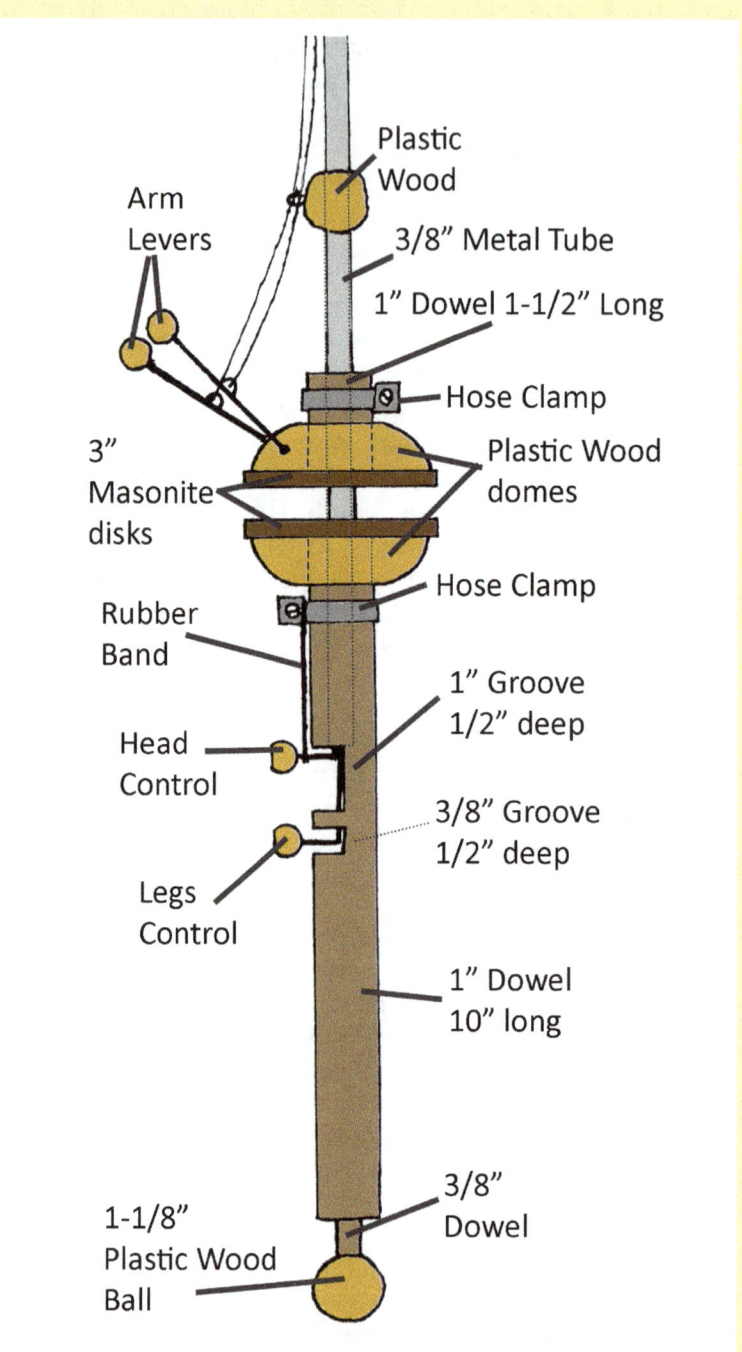

Fig. 44. Diagram of Myers' control handle.

drilled, the dowel rod would then be split with a bandsaw for the entire length the hole was drilled. This ensured the dowel could clamp tightly around a ⅜" metal tube. From the control handle to the top of the puppet, the ⅜" metal tube provided both the backbone support of the puppet as well as the necessary conduit for the leg and head mechanism rods. This tube is tightly secured into the control handle by a metal hose clamp.

Glued to the very top of this control handle is a 3" diameter disk made of Masonite (earlier puppets had disks of copper). The bond between the Masonite and the control rod is further strengthened by a dome of Plastic Wood. Myers poked holes into the Plastic Wood to increase its surface area. If this was not done, the Plastic Wood would dry on the outside but remain wet on the inside, making it not as secure of a bonding agent. By poking the holes, Myers ensured the Plastic Wood would dry and cure quickly and evenly. A shorter 1" diameter dowel has a ⅜" hole drilled all the way through and is sliced with the bandsaw just like the control handle. This shorter dowel also has a 3" Masonite disk glued (this time to the bottom) and a Plastic Wood dome to ensure its strength. The two disks are essential to keep the puppet upright at play-board level when the operator is not holding the puppet. There is enough room left between the disks to sandwich onto the shelf slot system.

Before the control handle is secured to the metal tube, the mechanisms for the feet and head must be completely set. The head and leg mechanisms are controlled through two separate buttons located on the control handle, and grooves were cut out to give the mechanisms room to move. Myers chiseled out a little more space for each of these mechanisms to move effectively.

For the leg mechanism, a metal control rod runs from between the legs of the puppet down inside the metal tube to the control handle. Near the top of the puppet's legs, Myers cut out a section of the metal tube, allowing the leg control rod to exit the tube. Around the cut, Myers reinforced the tube by wrapping it with Plastic Wood. The foot control rod was bent towards the front of the puppet and soldered to a separate metal cross-member rod. This cross-member went through a hole drilled in each of the pup

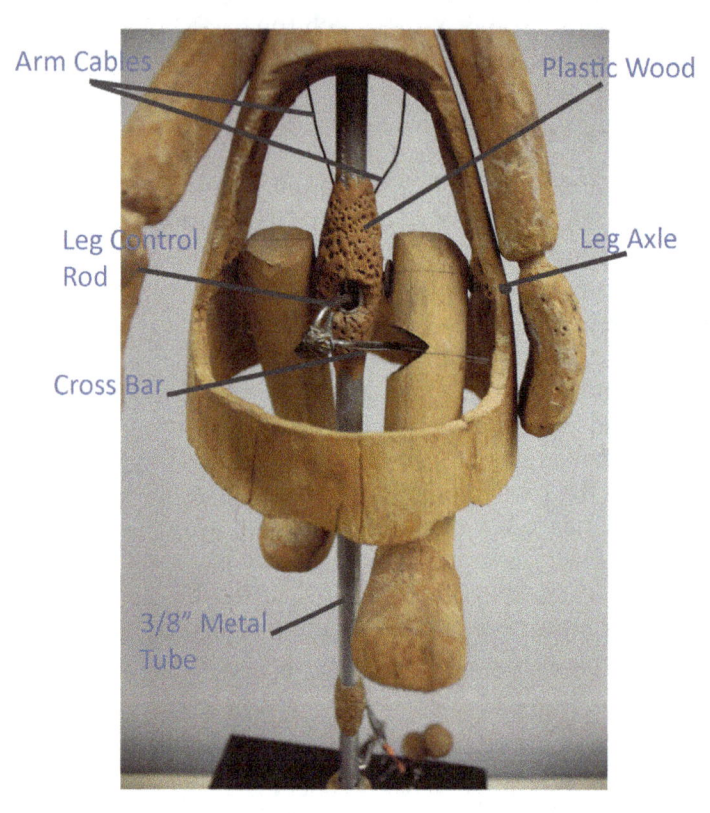

Fig. 45. Internal Mechanism
(Left Leg Stepping Forward &
Right Leg Moving Backward)
Front view.

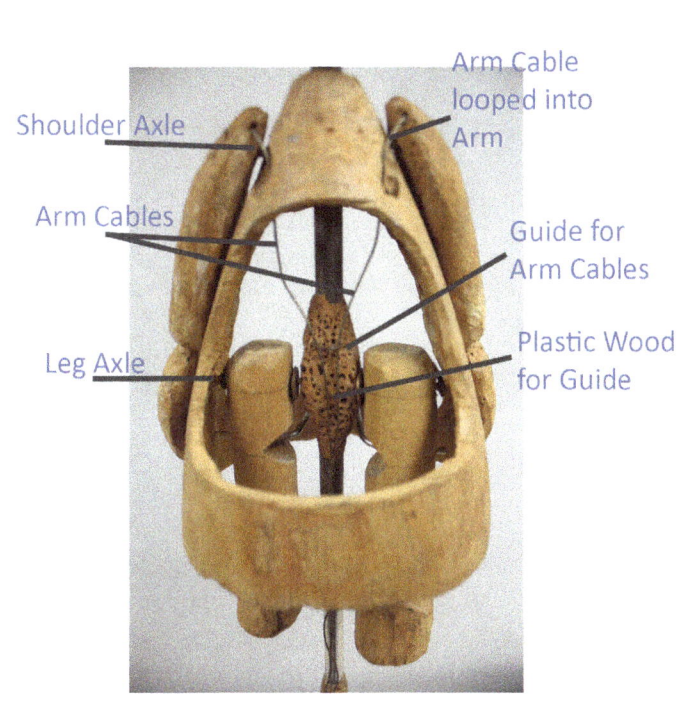

Fig. 46. Internal Mechanism
Back view.

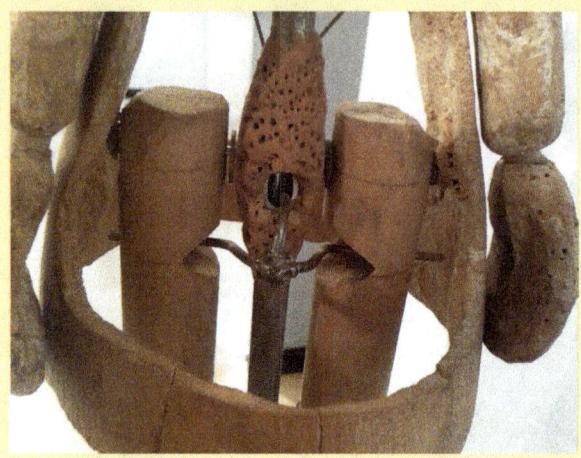

Fig 47. Closeup of Leg Mechanism.

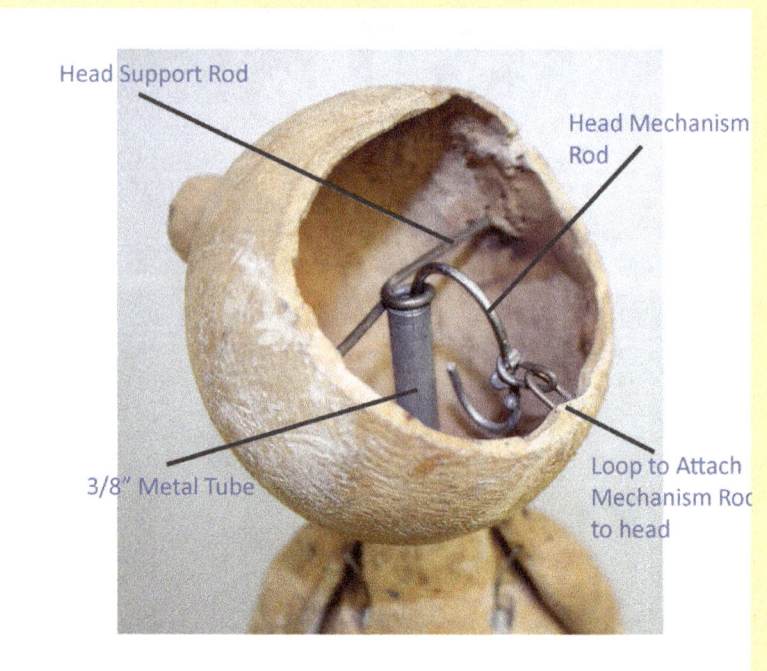

Fig. 48. Head Mechanism.

pet's legs. The puppet's legs are made of 1" dowels. Where the cross-member enters the legs, Myers carved away a slot in the leg, enabling the cross-member to rock back and forth with enough clearance. Above where the cross-member attaches to the legs, each leg is attached to the puppet through another rod. This rod is the axle for the legs so they can swing forward and backwards. Down at the puppet's control handle, the foot control rod is bent and spiraled into a Plastic Wood covered button. The puppet operator rocks the button right and left, tranmitting the action up the foot control rod, to the cross-member, and into the legs of the puppet. This movement ensures when the right foot moves forward, the left foot moves back, and vice-versa.

The head control rod extends from the top of the ⅜" control tube and is arched inside the puppet's head to a hook eye secured at the inner back of the puppet's head with Plastic Wood. The arch of the head mechanism rod must be precise because if it is done wrong, the head rod will seize up and not operate effectively. The ⅜" metal tube does not extend to the top of the puppet's head, but instead supports a separate rod in the very center of the head. This rod is attached to the lower cheeks of the puppet and extends up to the ⅜" metal tube (almost like a widened, upside-down "v"). The rod is twisted into a loop which rests on the very top of the ⅜" metal tube. The head control exits the tube and passes through the middle of that twisted loop to keep the head in place. The bottom of the puppet head has a slot just a little wider than the ⅜" metal tube, which ensures the head can move up and down smoothly, and only in the intended directions. The head control rod is bent into a button at the control handle, much like the foot control rod. The head control rod can move right, left, up and down, enabling the puppet's head to move in the same ways.

Both the head and the leg control rods are bent and looped out of the control handle. The loop is covered in Plastic Wood, creating a "button." A piece of sand paper is glued onto the Plastic Wood button to give an abrasive surface for the operator to easily control the puppet. I believe Myers set all of the mechanisms on the puppet first, then bent the control rods at the bottom. Only after this, would he have clamped the control handle into place.

The feet stay in a neutral position by gravity pulling downwards on the leg dowels; however, gravity works against the head control. If the head control does not have a return, the head would rest with the puppet looking at the ceiling. Myers discovered rubber bands make a great return to ensure the puppet's head is in neutral position and is facing forward. This rubber band wraps around both the head control button and the hose clamp used to secure the control handle to the ⅜" metal tube.

The arms of Myers' puppets are cable controlled. The arm control levers are located above the upper 3" disk which supports the puppet on the slotted shelf. Myers created a lever for each arm, and attached both to the puppet by placing a metal pin through the bottom of the levers before securing the pin with Plastic Wood. He incorporated the metal pin into the design of the Plastic Wood dome for the shorter upper dowel rod. The arm control levers are made of metal rods having a soldered bent "U" shaped rod attached. The end of the rod, where the operator pulls down, is covered with a Plastic Wood ball. Braided airplane cable is looped through the "U" shaped rod attached to each lever, and then soldered to itself. This cable runs up the outside of the ⅜" metal tube. Myers secured two hook eyes onto the metal tube (using Plastic Wood) to help guide the cables up the puppet; one is part way up the metal tube and the second was placed behind the cut made in the metal tube for the leg mechanism. The cables are routed through the puppet's body and out through crater shaped holes drilled behind the shoulders of the puppet. The holes are crater shaped to minimize snag and resistance on the cable.

Myers drilled two holes in the top of each of the puppet's arms. The top hole was drilled from the back of the arm, all the way through to the front. The second hole is drilled just under that top hole, and only goes about half way through the arm. Myers then channeled out a little Plastic Wood to bridge the holes together. The airplane cable enters the top hole from the back and threads through the arm. I believe Myers then applied Duco Cement to the tip of the cable, and placed it into the lower hole. He waited for the cement to dry before pulling back on the cable, allowing it to rest inside the channel that bridges the holes before he applied a little Plastic Wood over the cable, hiding it from the front.

The puppet's arms are attached to the puppet by a rod extending the entire width of the inside of the puppet. At each end of this rod, Myers soldered a washer and created a dome of solder. The smooth solder is what the Plastic Wood arm pivots on. From below, the operator pulls down on the arm levers, putting tension on the cable, pulling at the top of the arm and lifting the arm up. Gravity works as the natural return for the puppet's arms. If it was necessary to keep the arms up (such as in the ballroom dance with Geraldine and the Beast in *Beauty and the Beast*), Myers would create hooks the arm levers could rest in, allowing the puppet's arms to remain up and freeing the operator's hands to control other mechanisms.

In the coming chapters, I explore repairs made to the puppets and the sets which may give further insight to the technical aspects of Dick Myers' unique puppet shows.

From **Cinderella**.

Fig. 49. (*Left*) Short Clerk

Fig. 50. (*Above*) Tall Clerk

5

Restoration

Experimentations & Restorations of Audio Recordings

While many successful puppet shows utilized live voices in their performances, to more easily adapt to the audience's reactions, Dick Myers was one of the few who were able to perform to perfection with a prerecorded audio track of the entire show. During the early years of Myers' career, he worked with a few puppeteers who were beginning to experiment with the technique of using prerecorded voice and sound effects in their shows. However, most did not come close to perfecting the system like Myers would.

When Fay Coleman hired Myers as a puppeteer, he employed Myers' expertise in engineering and technology to create a prerecorded show. In 1950, commenting on his production of *Tom Sawyer*, Coleman wrote: "Using tape recording on dialogue, sound effects and music. It's a little early to tell whether we like it or not, but it's an interesting experiment."[1]

Within the field of puppetry, there were many other puppeteers experimenting with prerecorded audio. In 1951, Rufus and Margo Rose performed their long-anticipated production of *The Ant and*

the Grasshopper using prerecorded voice talents. In the following quote, Rufus Rose describes the process of working with audio that has been prerecorded for the show:

> We have recently produced *The Ant and the Grasshopper,* a musical fantasy, using tape recording for all voices, music and sound effects. Although we are not completely satisfied with this first attempt, we have learned much and believe the tape recorded method provides important advantages for achieving superior performances... From the beginning the tape recording method should be fully exploited for its real worth to the best possible show, which means:
>
> 1). The show must be written and recorded with extreme care for TIMING. You must rehearse the entire show including puppeteering and all other business before the final script is set and recorded in order to determine a pace that is dramatic and practical for the puppeteers.
>
> 2). The quality of voices, music and sound effects must be excellent, therefore all conditions for making the recording must be right. This suggests a sound studio with trained personnel. Use as many artists for voices as necessary to obtain best characterization...
>
> 3). Rehearsal and rehearsal with the recording is of utmost importance...more concentration and skill are called for than with an unrecorded show. The puppeteer must anticipate and act his puppet every instant...
>
> In conclusion, I believe that the tape recorded puppet show will find its proper place and that audiences and producers will share in the benefits which this new technique will afford. [2]

Both Coleman and the Roses experimented with prerecorded audio in their shows while Myers was under their employment. When Myers decided to record his first show, *Dick Whittington and his Cat,* he refined his recording techniques and surpassed many technological disadvantages which many prerecorded shows had previously experienced. The largest fault which occurred in pre-recorded puppet shows was the unpredictable audience reaction. Sometimes the audience would have a large reaction and cut off the next bit of dialogue. Other times, the audience would not react at all, leaving a quiet space in the dialogue where a reaction had been anticipated. Myers' solution to these issues was simple: he had a foot-powered pedal which would pause his reel-to-reel machine. The addition of the foot pedal served as one of the many revolutionary techniques Myers would pioneer for prerecorded puppet shows.

Through innovation, Myers sought out perfection for his shows; he wanted all the puppets' voices to be just as he envisioned them, so he recorded his own voice for every character. He realized he was not great with creating live voices, so he developed different sized cams and placed them within the reel-to-reel recorder. The cams would either speed up or slow down the speed at which the audiotape passed through the recording heads. A larger cam would slow down the tape while recording and would therefore play quickly during playback. This would make the voice talk faster and in a higher pitch than the original sound. These larger cams served in creating the voices of his female characters. A smaller cam would make the tape run quickly through the recording heads, and the tape would play back slower and lower pitched than the original.

Myers easily conquered the challenges he experienced with the tape's speed. He discovered when he was creating a female voice, he had to talk slowly in order for the voice to be understood during playback. This method would continue to be used throughout the remainder of his career. In recording these voices, he faced more challenges than just tape speed. Myers did not have the money to professionally record his shows and did most of the work at his home. Recording great quality audio can be a real challenge as everyday external noises (such as appliances, people in the other room, etc.) become quite clear in an audio recording. In order to create a nearly sound-free environment, Myers would record all of his audio sitting on the floor while tented by a blanket, with the microphone very close to his mouth. While audiences

would hear an array of manipulated vocals made up from Myers' own voice, they would very rarely hear the puppeteer's true voice. Primarily, Myers' normal voice would only be heard during the opening and closing audio narration for the performance.

Character voices only made up a small portion of Myers' show tapes; music would make up the majority. Most of the audio he used was from classical, jazz, and ragtime pieces. Myers would spend hours listening to records on a phonograph, taking notes of the moments in the music that he found interesting. When he knew which music he wanted to use for his show, he would then record it from the record onto his reel-to-reel machine. Having both the voices and the music, Myers would then take the time needed in working out the perfect timing of the entire show. He would cut and splice together every voice and music change, also splicing appropriate moments of silence in the show from a pre-recorded tape of "room sound". Myers' finished show tapes would sometimes have more than one hundred cuts and splices.

Prerecorded audio would prove to have great advantages for a one-man show. During this time, body microphones were impractical for performance. They were large and cumbersome, and had to be strapped around the neck, trailing along the umbilical. Most puppeteers who performed live audio would have a microphone on a stand which was stationary during the entire performance. This was sufficient for smaller houses, but in bigger venues, the audio would need to be turned up high (because the puppeteer was not always right next to the microphone), producing a "tin can" sound. However, a prerecorded show allowed for consistently clear audio, creating a perfect balance between voice and music.

At some point in Myers' career, he discovered a need to create "how-to" tapes for himself in which he would have the show reel-to-reel playing as he rehearsed while recording dictations of the entire blocking and scene transitions of the show. Myers would sometimes go months without performing one of his shows, so the tapes were an essential record for him to relearn each show. All four of his main shows had "how-to" tapes. However, Myers never created one for his experimental show, *Divertisement*, or his short show of vignettes, *Mall Show*.

Each of the four audiotapes was recorded on an open reel-to-reel tape, which is essentially a thin plastic band with ferric oxide bonded to it. Ferric oxide is similar to iron oxide, with only a slightly different chemical composition. Like iron oxide, ferric oxide can hold a magnetic charge when exposed to a specific magnetic field. Within a reel-to-reel machine's recording head are very tiny electromagnets that will magnetize the tape so it will play back the sounds initially recorded. When the physical tape is made, the ferric oxide is mixed with a bonding agent (glue) and also a dry lubricant to help ferric oxide remain on the plastic tape. Over time (decades), the tape will dry out, weakening the bonding agent and the dry lubricant so during playback there is a risk of the ferric oxide flaking off the plastic tape, losing the sound forever.

Myers' audio reel-to-reel tapes were at risk of the ferric oxide flaking off due to the age of the tapes. Most of the tapes were stored in metal containers, which had slowed the deterioration of the tape quality. Since these tapes were the only copies of his shows, it seemed necessary the restoration be handled by professional audio technicians. Though the tapes needed to be professionally digitized, I decided to research how this process would work.

The first issue I discovered was it could be difficult to keep the ferric oxide on the plastic of the magnetic tape. Since the bonding agent and the dry lubricant both can be brittle, they need to be reactivated. I found this could be achieved by baking the tapes in an oven at a low temperature. By heating the tape, any moisture buildup from over the years will be evaporated, making the bonding agent hold onto the plastic tape a little stronger. This technique would only provide a temporary solution, and in many cases will only allow a bad tape to be played once or twice. I further discovered tape splices on an old tape are also very delicate and brittle. Even baking the tapes may not preserve the glue on a tape splice. I found a weak splice meant it would need to be re-glued.

With all of the information, I knew the tape restoration would need to be put into the hands of a seasoned professional. After much research and discussions with various options, I shipped

the tapes off to Video Interchange, a company out of Maine which had been specializing in preserving audiotapes since 1978. The tapes were shipped out in June of 2012. Unfortunately, Bob Pooler, the owner and sole operator of Video Interchange, suffered some medical issues and in late September of 2012, the tapes were shipped back, untouched with a letter of apology. Suddenly, the time was running short and I needed to locate an audio digitization service which could work both quickly and efficiently while remaining within the budget.

The answer came quickly from a professor of acting at the University of Connecticut, Helen Kvale. She recommended a company out of Southington, Connecticut, called VSI Media. The company accepted the task of restoring the audio tapes. The restorations of the tapes were funded thanks to a generous grant bestowed to this project by the former Dean of Fine Arts, David Woods.

Fortunately, time was kind to all of Myers' reel-to-reel tapes.

Replacing a Broken Rope

Dick Myers' set pieces were efficiently constructed so they could lay down flat during touring and could easily be put together for performances. The pieces can be made 3-dimensional by using rubber bands and rope to hold them in position. During restoration, I replaced the rubber bands for all the set pieces for all four of Myers' shows. On the set of the fireplace from Cinderella's house I discovered the rope needed replaced (Fig. 51) The rope was broken close to where it was tied to the set piece. Luckily, the broken piece was saved by Myers. Therefore, I could replicate the new rope to look just like the original. The challenge soon came when I was unable to find the correct diameter of cotton rope to replace the original. The only rope available was in nylon, not cotton. Wanting to replicate original materials to the greatest possible extent, I decided it was time to learn how to make rope.

For this process, I needed to find cotton line that was 1/3 as thick as the broken rope. On my quest, I happened to see a chalk

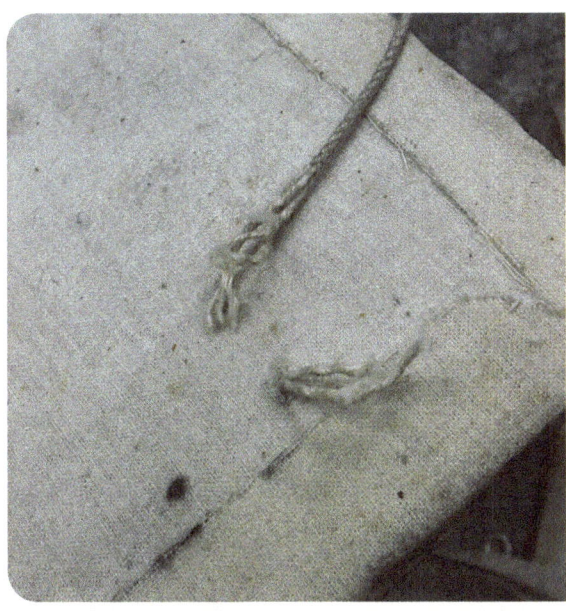

Fig. 51. Broken Rope

line in the tool cabinet. This chalk line was about 1/3 as thick as the original rope and made of cotton. I purchased a new spool of chalk line and proceeded to make the rope.

The process of making a rope consists of spinning each of the lines (three in this case) as tightly as possible in a clockwise direction. I fabricated three drill attachments to tie each of the cotton lines. I had to be constantly careful to ensure each of these strands was equally as tight as the next. Additionally, I was diligent in keeping a constant lateral tension on the rope strands once they were spun. Had they become too relaxed, the twisted strands would have clumped up and become unusable.

Before twisting the three strands, they needed to be secured on one end. For this to happen, I had put a screw into the end of a dowel and then clamped it into a vice. All three strands were then tied to the screw. Each strand of rope was tied to the drill attachments I had created. I was then able to spin each strand – one at a time. The home-made bit was put into the drill, which enabled the string to be wound very tight. (Fig. 52)

Fig. 52. Winding New Rope.

When all three strands were equally tight, I carefully placed all three drill attachments into the drill (Fig. 52) By spinning counterclockwise, the three strands twisted together creating a three-strand rope. The strands relaxed together, allowing their fibers to intertwine. While the rope was still attached to the drill, I rubbed a candle back and forth over the new rope to coat it with wax.

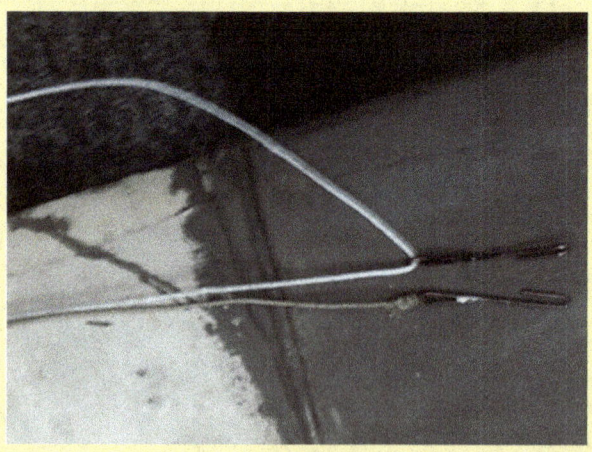

Fig. 53. Old and new ropes with wire hooks.

It was then time to find out how to remove the old rope without hurting the set piece. The old rope was wrapped around and tied to a metal rod. The loose end of the rope was then covered with a piece of glued muslin. The old rope was removed relatively easily with an X-acto knife. I carefully cut the rope off the metal rod and gently removed the end that was glued under the muslin.

I attached the rope without cutting out the metal rod. If I had cut out the metal rod, it would have been easier to tie the knot, but I wanted to make sure the repair was as minimally intrusive as possible on the set piece. I created a square knot much like the original knot, and carefully tucked it between the rod and the set piece.

I created a new hook as well so I could use the old rope and hook as a reference for the correct length. The old rope served as a guide for laying the new rope in place and provided precision on where to tie the new knot. (Fig. 53)

Once the repair process was completed, the set piece stood secure and looked as if though it had just graced the stage.

Missing Box Seats

When rehearsals for *Cinderella* began, I quickly discovered there were two missing identical set pieces. These were the box seats for the Counselor and the Page during the Prince's ball scene. Very few photos were taken of Myers' shows, but luckily there was one of this scene, which provided me with the size and colors which would be needed to accurately replicate the pieces. (Fig. 54)

Through a study of all the existing set pieces Myers had made, I could determine one possible design which Myers may have used. From the existing photo, I could use the puppets as size references to figure out the dimensions of the original boxes, which were ten inches by ten inches.

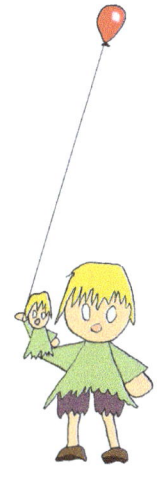

Fig. 54. Missing Spectator Boxes.

To begin the process, I laid out a piece of cardboard of the same thickness as the rest of the Dick Myers set pieces. Next, I measured out forty-two inches of cardboard (ten inches for each of the four sides of the box, plus a two inch overlap). At each of the ten-inch marks, I drew a line to reference where to fold the cardboard for a corner of the box. The measurement from the bottom to the top was found by measuring from the puppet support to the part of the puppet which was exposed to the camera in the photo.

Fig. 55. Checking New Spectator Box.

I made a nice crisp fold in the cardboard by rolling a spline roller along the line. This tool is designed to push in a rubber gasket which holds a window screen into its metal frame. In this case, it made a great tool to score the cardboard for the set piece. After all four lines were scored, I folded the cardboard into the desired three-dimensional shape: a box. The box was put in place on the stage to make sure it matched the size and height of the original. (Fig. 55)

For this set piece, I chose to use Dick Myers' rope and hook method to hold it together as a 3-dimentional unit. During this part of the process, I decided to use some of the extra rope which was left over from repairing one of the *Cinderella* set pieces as well as several hooks which I had made while learning Myer's soldering techniques.

All of Dick Myers' set pieces are made primarily of cardboard and muslin. Even his touring boxes were made of these materials. I learned if too much glue was applied, the cardboard would warp, so the glue was brushed on fairly thinly. Working quickly on only one side of the box at a time, I evenly brushed the glue, while trying to keep the glue from drying too quickly. Once the cardboard was covered with a thin layer of glue, the muslin was pulled tight and smoothed over the cardboard.

When the entire front side of the cardboard had muslin glued to it, I bent the cardboard into 90-degree angles and pulled up the extra fabric at those corners. Next, darts were cut in the overhanging muslin at each fold in the cardboard. This allowed me to pull the muslin a little tighter and wrap it around to the inside of the set piece. Instead of painting the glue onto the cardboard, I brushed a very thin coat onto the backside of the muslin then pulled the muslin tight and folded it over onto the box.

With the muslin adhered to the cardboard; it was time to stiffen the muslin by brushing four light layers of glue lightly onto the set piece, again making sure not to get it too wet (because the

cardboard underneath could otherwise warp). It was imperative, for the same reason, to let each layer dry before applying the next coat.

A major challenge was to find a way for the boxes to maintain their right-angled corners when they were made three-dimensional. One of Dick Myers' other set pieces offered a solution to this problem. The final pieces I used to complete the structure of the boxes were: a small wooden triangle which fit into each corner of the boxes and four rectangles which acted as guides and stoppers. (Fig. 56 and Fig. 57)

Fig. 56. Corner Brace Folded Flat.

Fig. 57. Corner Brace In locked position.

Myers used both muslin and glue to attach similar pieces on his own sets, so I followed his lead. It was important for these pieces to be able to not only lock into the 90 degree angle, but also to lie flat. When Dick Myers was done with one of his shows, all the set pieces needed to lie perfectly flat so they would take up the least amount of storage room. I created an attachment for the hook to hold onto, which allowed for the box to remain open or to collapse closed.

The next challenge was to replicate how the set pieces attached to the stage. I chose to use the most common Myers method. I was very familiar with this technique because of an earlier repair of a broken clip on the *Cinderella* fireplace set piece. One of the problems I experienced was the clothespin spring was not strong enough to keep the box up on its own. My solution was also inspired by a few of Dick Myers' existing set pieces. I drilled two holes on either side of the clip. I used a screw with a washer to be my anchor point. I was then able to loop two rubber bands through the holes and attach them to the screw, strengthening the spring of the clothespin. Carianne Hoff painted the boxes. Hoff was able to use the existing photos to match the design and color of the original missing pieces. Overall, the boxes for the Councilor and the Page turned out to be exact replications of Myers' original set pieces. (Fig. 58)

Fig. 58. Completed New Spectator Box.

Casting in Mend-All

Throughout the early and mid twentieth century, many puppeteers, especially Dick Myers, used a product called Plastic Wood to cast puppet parts. The majority of Myers' puppets were composed of this material. He did not like to work with fabric, and therefore chose to use Plastic Wood to cast the costumes as well as the heads, arms, hands, and feet. Although this material is very toxic, , little consideration or concern kept puppeteers from using it in the early to mid 20th century. The brand name of Plastic Wood still exists, but the product is made with different compounds and by a different company. In Myers' time, Plastic Wood was produced and distributed by Boyle-Midway Inc., a company which still exists and owns the product WD-40. Plastic Wood is now produced and distributed by DAP, with a formulated compound that has a lower viscosity than the original moldable Plastic Wood. Some puppeteers cast out of this new formulated Plastic Wood, but it lacks the tensile strength of the original. Fred Thompson, a Connecticut-based puppeteer, recommended I experiment with a product called Mend-All. This product serves as a wood filler with a formula closely resembling that of the old Plastic Wood. I decided to create a Myers-style shoe out of this material, with the hope of having a better understanding of this old casting process.

I sculpted a replica of a Myers-style shoe out of oil based clay. Dana Samborski, a masters student at the University of Connecticut's Puppet Arts Program, created a plaster mold for me. After cleaning the residual clay out of the mold, I submerged both halves under water. Soaking the mold in water will prevent the Mend-All from curing to the plaster. Also, allowing the Mend-All to cure underwater minimizes the potent and unhealthy smell of the chemicals. This technique of using water as the mold release was first introduced to puppeteers by Rufus Rose.

The plaster molds were submerged under water overnight for twelve hours. I observed the mold's release of air. (Fig. 59) Once a mold is no longer producing air bubbles, it is ready to be used

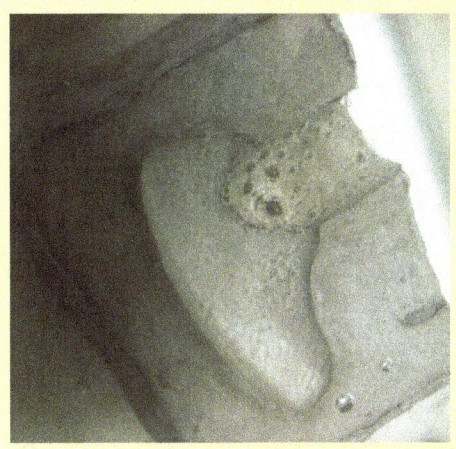

Fig. 59. Air bubbles from submerged plaster mold.

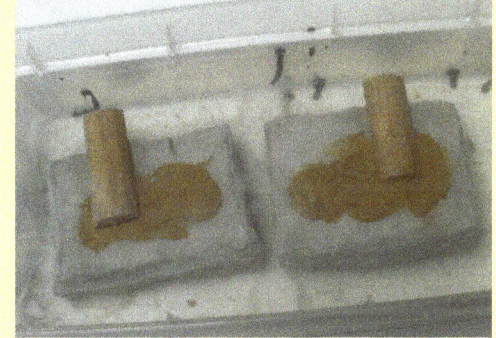

Fig. 60. Mold with Mend-All immersed in water bath.

for casting. Air bubbles are a problem in casting because they will push up against the Mend-All, pulling it away from the mold and distorting the cast.

While working with Mend-All, it is recommended to wear latex gloves. Mend-All, while not as toxic as Plastic Wood (containing both acetone and toluene), has a high level of acetone which can cause skin irritation. I also used a vent hood to pull out many of the toxic inhalants found in Mend-All.

Fig 61. Drying demolded Mend-All castings.

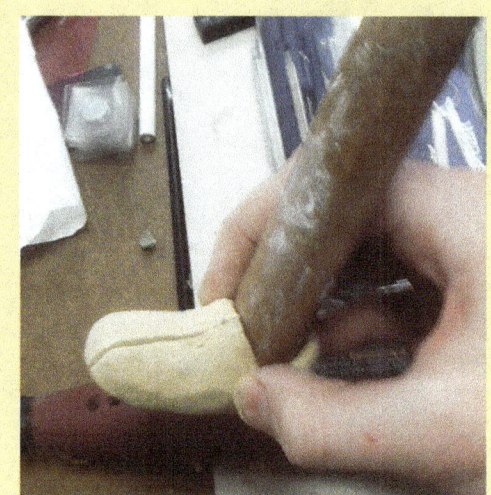

Fig 62. Dry Fitting Shoe to leg.

Fig. 63. Completed shoe ready for painting.

I created a pancake of Mend-All, pushed it into the mold, pressing a very thin layer of it against the insides of the mold. A dowel coated with petroleum jelly (representing the leg of the puppet) was pressed into the ankle area of the mold and the Mend-All lined molds were once again submerged in water to prevent many of the odorous chemicals from dispersing in the air. I let these remain underwater for about twelve hours before removing the Mend-All from the mold. (Fig. 60)

The Mend-All cast was easily removed from the mold. (Fig. 61) The excess flashing, the "Mend-All" not intended to be part of the cast, was easily removed with a sharp X-acto knife. These two halves of the shoe were penetrated with water and needed to dry. I placed them on a paper towel atop a rubber tile so the water would not hurt the desk below.

With the flashing removed, I used Duco Cement to adhere the two sides. Also, since the foot needed to be attached to a dowel, I made sure the dowel was in position within the shoe before gluing (Fig. 62). Mend-All is a compound which bonds to itself unnoticeably. Therefore it was the best product to use to seam and smooth out several imperfections on the cast shoe.

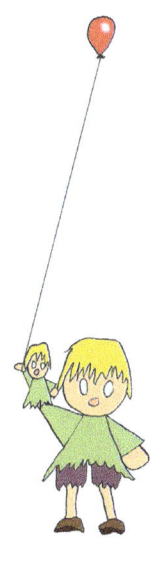

Fig. 64. Dog's Broken Tail.

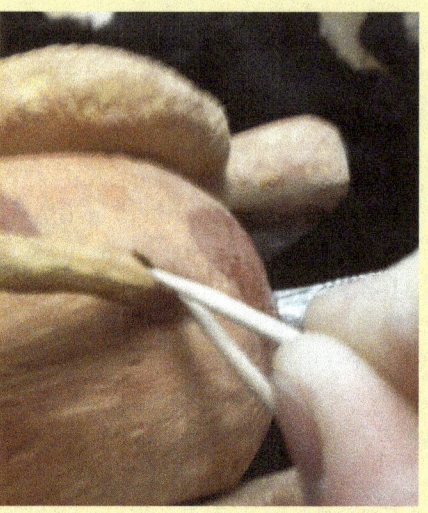
Fig. 65. Applying Duco Cement with toothpick.

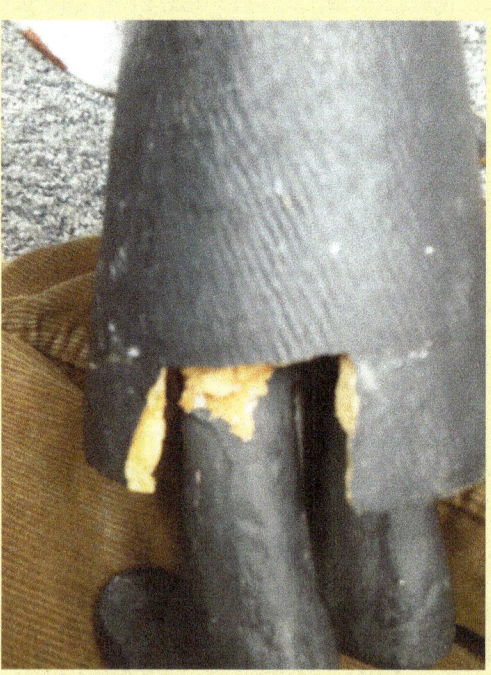
Fig. 66. Missing section of Knight's tunic.

Mending Plastic Wood with Duco

There were several puppets in the Dick Myers collection which needed simple repairs due to cracked or broken pieces of Plastic Wood. (Fig. 64) In my research, I found the recommended adhesive for bonding Plastic Wood to itself was Duco Cement. Unlike Plastic Wood, Duco Cement is still being manufactured and works as well now as it did decades ago. Duco Cement softens the Plastic Wood, allowing the two pieces to fuse back together.

How to use Duco Cement to make a Plastic Wood repair:

1. Clean and prep both surfaces to be bonded. I used rubbing alcohol to get off any oils, etc. Allow the cleaning agent to dry completely before proceeding to the next step.

2. Apply a very thin layer of Duco Cement to both surfaces that will be bonded together and wait until it is dry (approximately 5 minutes). I used very little Duco Cement on the tip of a toothpick. Wedging another toothpick into the cracked Plastic Wood to open up the gap, allowed me to work freely to apply the Duco Cement to both sides of the repair.

3. Reapply Duco Cement to one of the surfaces and pinch together. I held the two pieces tightly together for about ten minutes. If I had been able to clamp the pieces, it would have been ideal because clamping would cause consistent pressure, making sure the bond did not break. Unfortunately, the nature of these repairs made clamping impossible due to lack of space for a clamp.

Restoring a Knight Costume

When I assessed Myers' puppets, they were for the most part in wonderful condition, however repairs were necessary on some puppets. The Knight from Cinderella was missing a piece of Plastic Wood which served as part of its tunic. (Fig. 66). A search

Fig. 67. Sculpted Clay Model of missing piece of tunic.

Fig. 68. Attaching new piece with Mend-All.

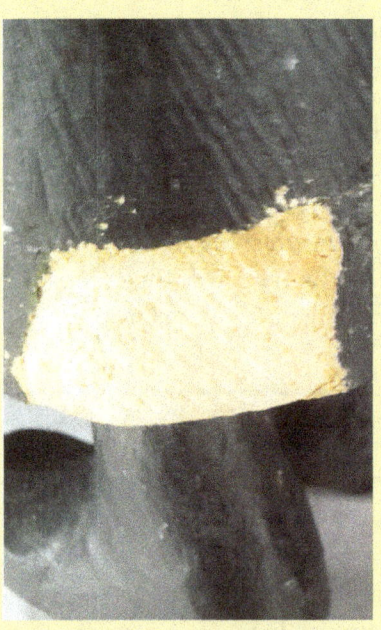

Fig. 69. Ready for painting.

through each of the boxes in which the Dick Myers' collection was stored did not turn up the missing piece. I knew there were several possible ways to approach this repair, but wanted to find the best way to minimize any chance of mistakes.

My inspiration for this repair (although a long way from puppetry) came from my understanding of restoration work being done to the Parthenon in Athens, Greece. Led by a group of masterful architects, the restoration aims to repair all the marble work destroyed over the centuries. The architects' restoration technique consisted of creating pieces of marble which fit as perfectly as the missing pieces of the old marble columns.

In the same respect, I sculpted a piece of clay into the missing area of Plastic Wood. Through the use of clay, I was able to match the lined texture of the original Plastic Wood exactly. Plastic wrap was used as a barrier between the clay and the old Plastic Wood. This technique ensured the integrity of the puppet was left intact and prevented clay residue from remaining on the puppet. (Fig. 67)

I created a plaster mold and cast using Mend-All. This method had additionally been used in casting Cinderella's shoe. With the new piece pulled from the mold, I spent a few hours sanding and dry fitting the new piece so it became the perfect thickness to fit onto the puppet. I then cleaned the old Plastic Wood, making sure there was no dirt to hinder the bond of the new piece.

Instead of using Duco Cement to bond the piece onto the puppet, I decided it would be better to use Mend-All. During this part of the process, I made sure to sand a little extra off the new piece so there was room for the Mend-All as a bonding agent. A thin layer of Mend-All was applied directly onto broken edges of the old Plastic Wood on the puppet, and then the cast piece of Mend-All was carefully fitted into place. (Fig. 69)

Puppet Arts student Carianne Hoff was trusted to paint to match the original color. She has a great skill in paint mixing and color matching. She painted the repair with such exactness that it looks like it has always been a part of the original puppet.

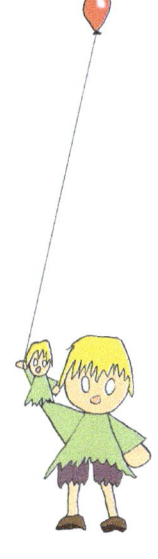

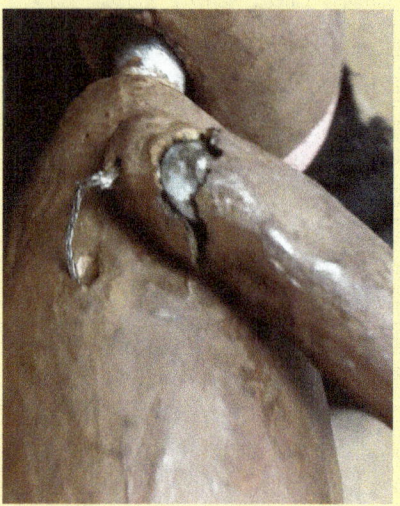

Fig. 70. Fred's Broken Arm.

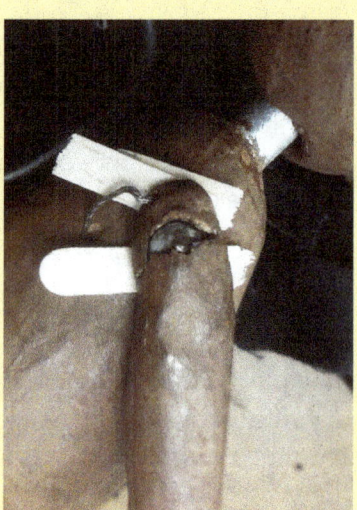

Fig. 71. Splints

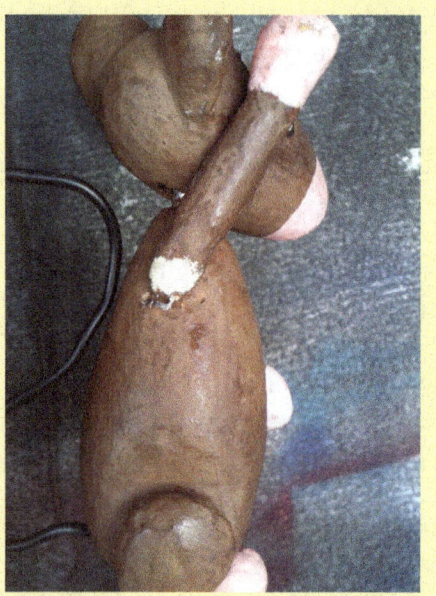

Fig. 72. Applied Plastic Wood.

Repairing a Broken Arm

Fred (the mouse from the show *Cinderella*) had a broken arm, which was one of the most difficult repairs to carry out. "Fred's" mechanized arm had broken at the pivot point. (Fig. 70) The arm had snapped in two and was barely hanging on by a small piece of wire used to control the arm. Looking closer at the broken arm, I noticed Myers had sculpted the Plastic Wood around an armature (instead of making a mold and cast). The arm pivoted on a domed piece of solder. Upon closer observation, I noticed Myers had connected the two pieces by soldering a washer onto the end of a metal rod and then made a smooth dome of solder for the arm to pivot.

To ensure no paint would be damaged on the puppet during the repair process, I made sure it was resting on a soft, thick piece of fabric. When the two pieces of arm were matched up, a small but noticeable piece of Plastic Wood was missing. I used Duco Cement to bond the two pieces of Fred's arm together. Without the missing piece of Plastic Wood, aligning and holding the two pieces together was very difficult. To ensure the arm would remain in the correct position as the Duco Cement dried, I created splints out of a coffee stir stick to hold the arm in place. (Fig. 71)

The missing piece of Plastic Wood had been there for more than just appearance. After the Duco Cement dried, the arm still did not work properly. It would twist and seize, and only raise to about 1/3 the height it should have. During the replacement process, I carefully added Plastic Wood back to the arm in a way which would enable it to function as intended. First, the area was prepared by sanding the paint off of the arm where the new material would need to bond. I knew one of the problems to avoid was having the new Plastic Wood stick to the solder dome the arm pivots on. Therefore, I decided to use Petroleum Jelly as a barrier between the solder and the new Plastic Wood. The challenge here was to only apply the petroleum jelly to the metal and not get any on the Plastic Wood. Otherwise, there was a risk of the new Plastic

Fig. 73. Broken Arm Wire.   Fig. 74. Two holes for Wire.

Fig. 75. New Arm Wire in place.

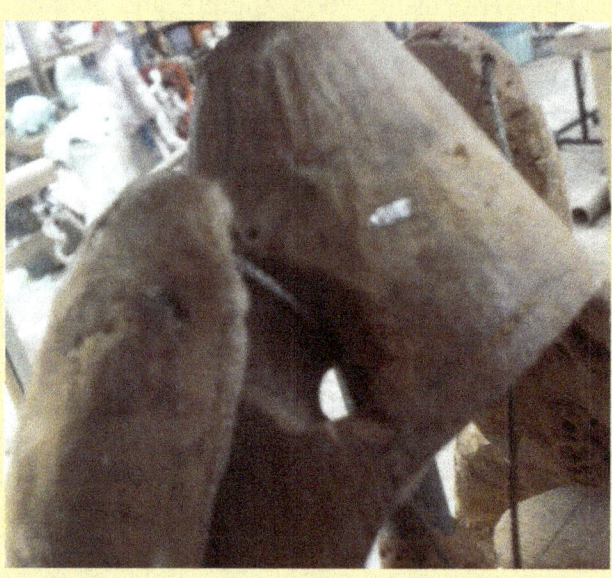

Wood not sticking to the old. Fortunately, I was eventually able to achieve my aim by lightly coating the solder while moving the arm up and down.

Carefully, the new Plastic Wood was smoothed to fill in the missing piece. I applied two layers of Plastic Wood to the break; each one was about as thin as an eggshell. (Fig. 72) After the first layer had been applied, I carefully moved the arm up and down over the pivot point. I did this every fifteen minutes for 2 hours, ensuring the Plastic Wood did not stick to the solder while making sure the arm's range of motion was correct. Once the second layer had dried, I tested the arm's mechanism and range of motion. After the repair process was completed, the arm began to perform as expected. To finish off the repair process, Carianne Hoff matched the paint and blended the repair with the original puppet, making the difference nearly imperceptible.

Replacing a Broken Arm Wire

The arms of a Dick Myers style puppet are controlled by a simple, hand made cantilever. When this lever is pulled down, the wire tightens and in the process lifts the arm. Though this wire is made of metal, it unfortunately can weaken over time causing it to break. The breakage in the metal wire led to the repair of a few of Myers' puppets. (Fig. 73) The wire he had used consisted of a flexible, braided, thin-gauged wire with a monofilament core. This wire was manufactured for the aeronautical field and sold as airplane cable. However, I was unable to find any company who currently manufactures wire of this design.

To begin the repair, the frayed broken end of the wire was trimmed to prevent abrasions on my hands from the frayed metal ends as this repair continued. I drilled out the remnants of the broken wire that Myers had looped through two holes in the arm. (Fig. 75) In order to ensure the holes were clear of debris, a drill bit one size bigger than the diameter of the wire was used. Once

Fig. 76. Soldering Arm Wire to Control Lever.

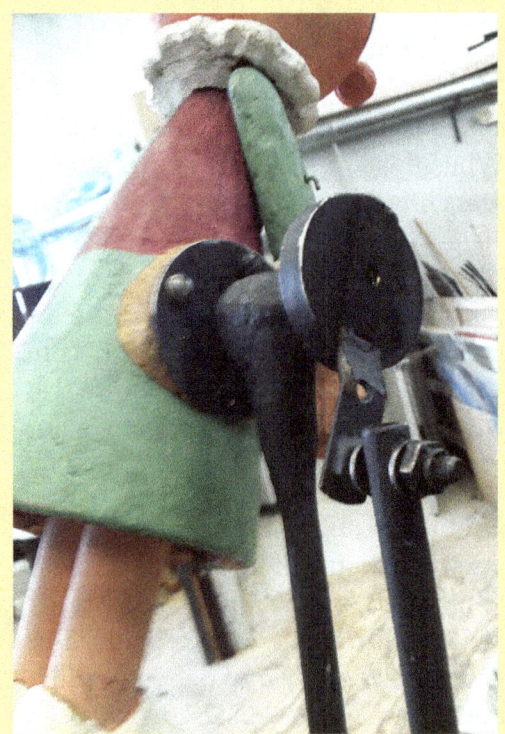

Fig. 77. Trampoline Mechanism.

the arm holes were prepped, I needed to remove the wire from the lever below. The wire was looped through this lever and then soldered together. In some repairs, the loop of the wire was very large and I was able to shorten it, reusing the original wire. However, in other repairs, I created an extension to the original wire because there was an insufficient length of wire remaining on the puppet. In order to remove the old wire, I reheated it with a soldering iron. This process allowed the old solder to let go slowly, which enabled me to remove the wire from the lever.

With the wire removed from the lower lever, I was then able to feed the wire through the two holes I had drilled into the puppet's arm. I had coated the end of the wire with Duco Cement before pushing it into the final hole to ensure it tightly bonded to the Plastic Wood. Once the Duco Cement was dry, I lightly pulled on the wire, moving the arm and ensuring the wire would hold.

I re-soldered the lower section of the wire. Next, I looped the wire back into the lever and used the other side as a reference for the final position of the lever. The lower portion of the wire was wrapped in a thin single-stranded wire to hold it together. Once it held on its own, I used the soldering iron to heat the wire and melt solder onto the lower portion of the wire (Fig.76). In Myers' design he had used a 60/40 rosin core solder (a spool was still within his supplies). In order to remain true to his original design, I used the same solder.

Silencing a Squeaking Acrobat

While rehearsing, I found the Trampoline Acrobat from *Cinderella* began to develop a squeak, which soon turned into physical difficulty with consistent puppet manipulation. The puppet's mechanism would need to be dismantled and re-lubricated. (Fig. 77) The mechanism was easy to take apart. I loosened a small hex-screw which locked the outer portion of the mechanism onto the main shaft. Once removed, the entire mechanism slid apart.

I was then able to see how the mechanism worked. It did not have bearings as I had originally thought. The mechanism was comprised of a metal sleeve which fit over a metal rod. The hole on the sleeve was very close to the same size as the rod, but loose enough so they could spin freely on the axis without any wobble. The grease that acted as a lubricant had now dried up, and was acting as an abrasive between the two pieces of metal. New axle bearing grease was carefully applied to both the sleeve and the rod with a cotton swab. I did not want to risk any of the grease touching the paint of the puppet, therefore the entire puppet (except the mechanism) was wrapped in plastic.

With both the sleeve and the rod now coated with grease, I slid the mechanism back together. Once together, the mechanism moved freely without any squeaks or difficulty of movement. While the newly-greased acrobat moved with gracious fluidity, it also presented a new performance challenge: precision and controllability. With these new challenges, I had to relearn throughout rehearsal how to manipulate the acrobat without the once-given resistance.

---

[1] Coleman, Fay. *Puppet Journal*. Volume 1 Issue 5. Pg 13. "Here 'n There". 1950.

[2] Rose, Rufus. *Puppet Journal* V2 Issue 5. Pg 10-11. "The Tape Recorded Puppet Show". 1951.

6

Exhibit

To fulfill a portion of the design aspect of my MFA, I accepted Dr. John Bell's invitation to curate the Ballard Institute and Museum of Puppetry's exhibit dedicated to Dick Myers' life and works in the field of puppetry. This proved to be a welcoming challenge and an opportunity for me to further examine and research the puppetry of Myers. For this exhibit, I wanted to include multiple aspects of his career in puppetry; therefore, I decided to dedicate almost as much time to researching as I did to restoring and rehearsing the shows. The exhibit covered Myers' work for the Stevens (Martin and Olga) and the Roses (Rufus and Margo), as well as his early hand puppet show, *The Magic Potion*. In the exhibit, I displayed some of the many technologies he had built by hand. These technologies served in representing the ways in which technology was an important aspect of his life. Additionally, the exhibit included displays on three of his solo shows that have yet to be remounted: *The Story of Dick Whittington, Simple Simon,* and *Divertisement.*

Myers' mechanized puppets have a unique design which made them impractical to put on view using the traditional puppetry display units at the museum. With this in mind, I designed and

Fig. 78. Setting up one of the display booths.

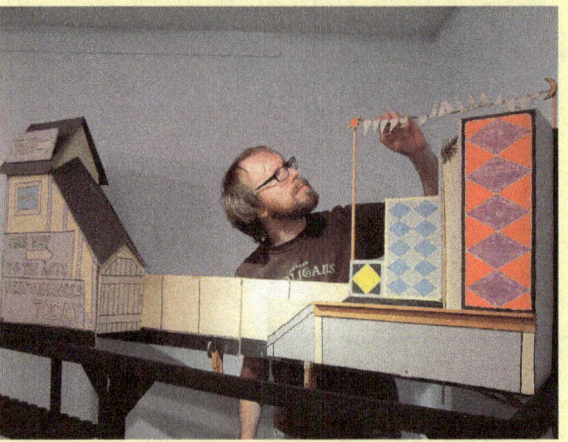

Fig. 79. Installing a set on a display booth.

Fig. 80 *Simple Simon* Fair scene on a display booth.

cutoms built display units to hold the puppets appropriately. I chose to design and build the exhibit in a compactable style which would allow it to be easily toured around the world. The main units were four foot tall versions of Myers' puppet booth. Figure 78 is from the beginning process of the museum installation.

When designing the displays for each of his shows, I decided to set up the main set pieces and display most of each show's cast in front of it. The scenery was clipped onto a scenery bar fastened to the back of the puppet booth.

Fig. 80 is the main display of Myers' *Simple Simon.* I designed the placement of the puppets in a "curtain call" fashion. The puppets on display from left to right are: Pie Man, Guard, Mariamne, Walter the Chicken, Simple Simon,   The King, Bad Man, Bad Woman, and Two Spectators.

Fig. 81 *The Story of Dick Whittington* cast and London set.

Fig. 82 *Divertisement* puppets in exhibit.

Fig.81 shows the curtain call scene set for *The Story of Dick Whittington.* The characters from left to right are: the Sea Captain, Alice, the Housekeeper, Dick's Cat, Dick Whittington, the Page, the King's Magician, the Farmer, and the Traveler.

The third booth I built displayed puppets from Myers' experimental piece, *Divertisement.* Due to the lack of information on this piece, the puppets could not be labeled with character descriptions. (Fig. 82)

Fig. 83. The Captain and Cat sail away. *The Story of Dick Whittington*.

Fig. 84. Commedia dell'arte puppets. *Divertisement*.

Fig. 85. The Boxers from *Simple Simon*.

During the show *The Story of Dick Whittington,* Myers used a miniature version of the Captain and the Cat to sail across the seas. (Fig. 83) This delightful piece was placed on display near the "curtain call" of *The Story of Dick Whittington.* Directly below the Captain and the Cat, I placed a book full of rare photos and documents for the patrons to look through. This book gave patrons the opportunity to experience further insight into Myers' career.

These *Commedia dell'Arte* influenced figures may have had a part in Myers' *Simple Simon.* While the script does not support this theory (and the puppets were found in a box labeled for *Divertisement*), I found a photo with the center puppet interacting with other *Simple Simon* puppets. (Fig. 84)

Fig. 85 is the two Boxers featured in one of the fair events in *Simple Simon.* In contrast to Myers' usual technically-mechanized puppets, these two boxer puppets are simple in design and control. In fact, these puppets have no movable parts, and rely solely on the puppeteer's manipulation skills and the audience's imagination. I designed and built the puppet stand to have an open bottom to display the lack of mechanisms.

In the production of *Simple Simon*, there are several versions of Simple Simon and Mariamne. While I was not able to display many puppets from the show, I thought these versions of Simon and Mariamne were worth the effort and challenge to display. (Fig. 86)

There were also multiple versions of the Bad Man and the Bad Woman. Figure 86 shows the mechanized dancing versions of these puppets. Myers had a removable tracking system which would attach to the play board and allow for the puppet mechanism to rest into the track. Once in place, the puppets could be pulled back and forth, appearing as if they were dancing a tango. (Fig. 87)

Fig. 86. Simon and Mariamne *Simple Simon*.

Fig. 87. Bad Man and Bad Woman dance a tango.

Fig. 88. Simon's Parents.

Simple Simon began with a worldwide classic image of a man and woman sitting in rocking chairs. The puppets were the calm-natured parents of Simon. Again, I chose to display to the patrons the mechanisms of the puppets, showing the complexity and skill that went into the puppets' creation. (Fig. 88)

Every one of Myers' shows featured a musician puppet in a baby bonnet. Baby William was well-remembered by Myers' fans, who anticipated the puppet's appearance in each of Myers' new productions. In *Dick Whittington and His Cat*, Baby William plays the violin. In *Cinderella*, he plays the piano (not displayed). In *Beauty and the Beast*, he plays the xylophone (not displayed). By the time *Simple Simon* premiered, Myers had created several more Baby William puppets playing instruments including violin, accordion, and trombone (not displayed). Additionally, Myers built Baby William, the Stage Manager of the Fair (the figure without an instrument). *Divertisment* featured Baby William several times, and also introduced him playing the harmonica. (Fig. 89)

Myers would sometimes offer demonstrations in conjunction with a performance. He had built a puppet with large pieces of Plastic Wood removed in order to expose the mechanisms. This puppet was a significant piece to display, not only because of its history, but also as a means for patrons to closely observe the complexity of Myers' mechanisms.

In addition to Myers' unique puppets, I also put on display the materials needed to create one of these puppets. Included was one of the slot boards used to hold a puppet during a production, the dowel rods used to create the handles of the puppets (Myers already cut and drilled these rods to be fit to his next puppet), and the round pieces of masonite which he cut for the disks used to hold the puppets up on the slotted shelf.

I also featured a few pieces of the electrical equipment Myers used during his shows. On the left is one of two audio reel-to-reel machines which would play the audio recording of the entire show

Fig. 89. Baby William and some of his musical instruments.

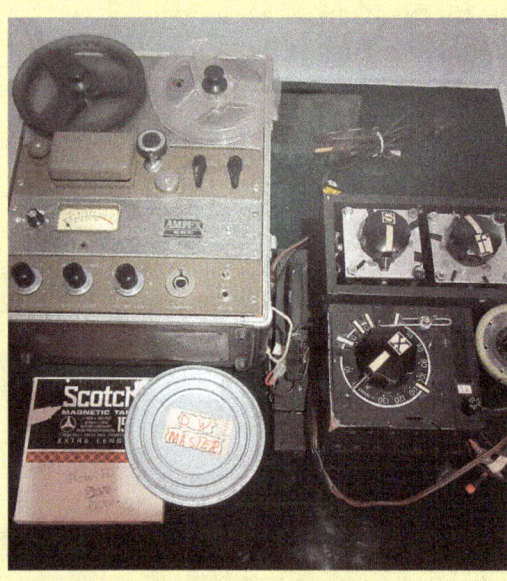

Fig. 90. Myers' tape recorder and lighting panel.

while Myers performed the puppets. Directly below the machine are two audio reels for *The Story of Dick Whittington*, one of the performance tape, and the other is the *How-To* tape. Displayed to the right of the reel is Myers' early lighting board which he had used for his shows. The light board weighs about twenty pounds. Each of the knobs controls a portion of the lights on his puppet booth. The later, lighter aluminum lighting board was not put on display.(Fig. 90)

I did not want to create an exhibit without including Myers' early work as a puppeteer and was lucky to unexpectedly come across some of his earliest puppets. While unsuccessfully searching the archives at the Ballard Institute and Museum of Puppetry for a small projector which was donated with a robot/puppet and was wanted for a different museum exhibit, I instead discovered a box labeled "Magic Potion." Knowing Myers had created a show titled *The Magic Potion* (which premiered at the 1950 Festival of the Puppeteers of America), I decided to open the box and examine the puppets. Included in the box was a script which had Myers' sense of humor, as well as Myers' distinct character voices written out. Allelu Kurten confirmed these were indeed Myers' puppets; she had thought she had given these puppets to a friend in California, but instead had donated them to the museum - a lucky mistake for the Myers museum exhibit. (Fig. 5)

Myers' work on the Rose-Stevens films was a significant influence in his later work. Luckily, the Ballard Institute and Museum of Puppetry had puppets from one of these films. Here are a few puppets from *The Ant and the Grasshopper*. Unfortunately, the film has not been located at this time, but thankfully the puppets have survived. (Fig. 91)

The puppets in Figure 92 were built by Martin Stevens as replicas of characters from *The Toymaker*, the second film that Myers worked on with the Rose-Stevens Films. They were created by Stevens for puppeteer Allelu Kurten so she could perform the script if she ever wanted to.

Fig. 91. *Ants and the Grasshopper* by Rufus and Margo Rose

Fig. 92. Spots and Stripes from *The Toymaker* by Martin and Olga Stevens.

Fig. 93. Seth with Marc Anthony from Martin and Olga Stevens' *Cleopatra*.

Fig. 94. Official opening of the exhibit. Seth at left, UConn President Susan Herbst in middle, Dr. John Bell at right, and Lindsay Simon behind.

I led two large group tours through the exhibit. Although I had prepared a short dedication video on the life and work of Myers for the exhibit, I did not show it during the tour. I was given the opportunity to further discuss the work of Myers in a forum and talkback which occurred immediately after the tours and provided an appropriate opportunity to debut this video titled, *And Now, the Entertainment.*

The documentary featured parts of interviews I had conducted. The interviewees in the film included Johan Vandergun, Allelu Kurten, Paul Vincent Davis, and Luman Coad. The video also had portions of a rare interview with Myers himself, which was part of a short video entitled, *Dick Myers: Master Puppeteer.* The video of Myers was taken near the end of his life by Cambiz A. Khosravi, a videographer based in Woodstock, New York, who granted me verbal permission to include part of his video in my documentary, *And Now, the Entertainment.* Unfortunately, Khosravi's twenty-one minute video is one of two surviving film/video featuring Myer's work which I uncovered over the process of this book. The other is a nearly four minute section in Philipe Genty's documentary *Marionettes de Tous les Pays* which was filmed at the 1972 UNIMA Congress in Charleville-Mezierres.

My work on the exhibit was not limited solely to the museum. In order to better advertise the museum and the Myers exhibit, I set up a display from *Simple Simon* at the Jorgenson Theatre. This display, along with promotional materials, was on view for thousands of patrons of the Connecticut Repertory Theatre's summer season. In the display were a few of the puppets which were not included in the exhibit at the Ballard Institute and Museum of Puppetry.

Overall, my role as curator for this exhibit provided a rich understanding of Myers' history and personal life experiences which influenced the unique puppeteer he came to be. This process enhanced my knowledge as a performer of his work, and allowed me to further connect with his mannerisms and witty sense of

Fig. 95. View of the exhibition gallery at the Ballad Institute and Museum of Puppetry.

Fig. 96. Another view of the exhibit.

humor. Furthermore, my research as the exhibit curator, and my thorough investigation of all aspects of Myers' life helped me to design an exhibit portraying his life and works in a way he hopefully would have approved.

Fig. 97. Farmer and Traveller from *The Story of Dick Whittington*.

Fig. 98. Seth demonstrating Guital Player from *Cinderella*.

Fig. 99. Dick Whittington and Cat.

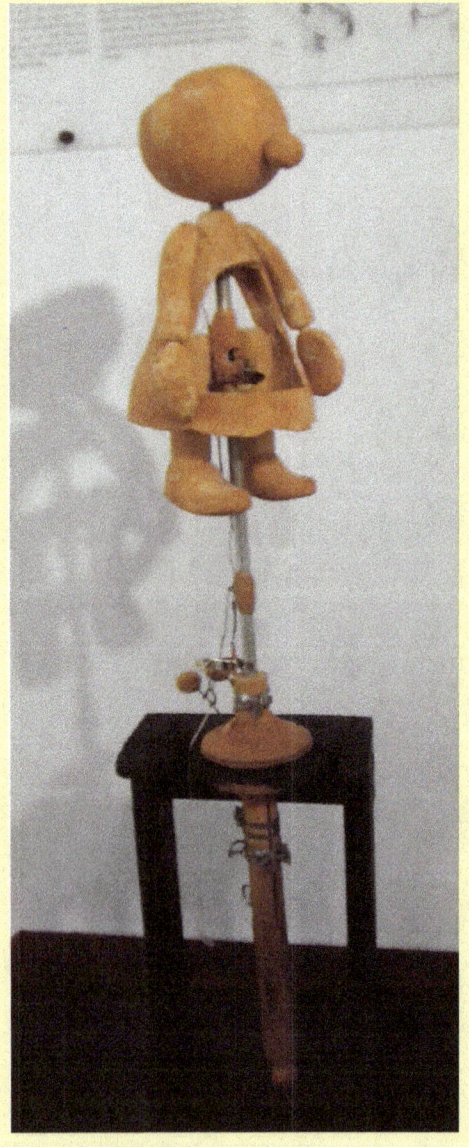

Fig. 100. Cut-away puppet showing Myers' rod mechanisms.

7

Rehearsal & Performance

In planning the rehearsal schedule for this project, I knew the process would require hours of diligent work. Throughout the rehearsal process, I was sure to set specific rehearsal days and times. This helped keep the show length consistent and allowed time to workshop and refine specific scenes. My rehearsals were four hours in length and scheduled for seven days a week. Depending on my availability during each day, I would sometimes double up a morning and evening rehearsal. Collaboratively, rehearsals were under the direction of Bart Roccoberton with assistance in choreography from Rachel Roccoberton Griffin. Described throughout this section are several stages of the rehearsal process, including pre-rehearsal assessments, beginning rehearsal preparations, presented challenges, workshop/possibilities, solutions, and the ultimate culmination of the project: the performances.

Beginning the pre-rehearsal process, I anticipated the handling and assessment of the puppets, sets, and stage. The shows were fairly well organized and had remained within their original touring boxes constructed by Myers. Each show had a set of boxes which housed the puppets and miscellaneous rods, racks, and props. I was rather fortunate these puppets were already

Fig. 101. "How does this fit together?"

Fig. 102. "This goes here."

Fig. 103. "Will there be enough light?"

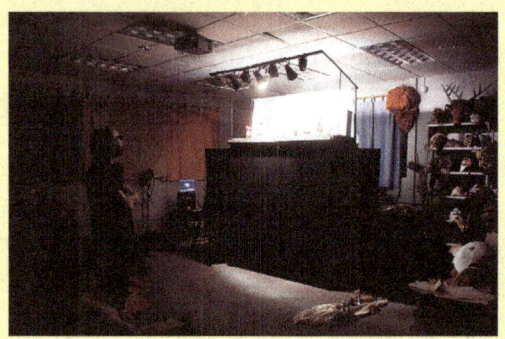

Fig. 104. "Are they all working?"

organized to an extent; otherwise it would have been a lot more difficult to learn which puppets went with what show. However, two shows were not in their original assigned boxes. At some point Myers had combined the puppets from *Divertisement* and *Cinderella* into the same boxes. Fortunately, these two shows were drastically different in both construction and painting style and it was easy to determine what puppets were from which show. Once I had finished cleaning and assessing the collection, it was time to learn how to reconstruct Myers' puppet booth.

At first I had thought the Myers' puppet booth would be simple to assemble. However, this assemblage turned into a several day process. The booth was like a puzzle. The initial frame for the booth was fairly easy to assemble; it consisted of six stackable units which only fit together one way. But figuring out the next part of the process, the lights and the cyclorama, proved to be more complex. Although Myers kept detailed notes on many aspects of his work, there were very few notes on how the puppet booth went together (and many of Myers' diagrams and notes had not yet been discovered when I was in this part of the process). Fortunately, many of the seemingly-random items found in Myers' boxes had sticky notes in reference to their purposes. With a little time, I was able to hang the light bar, position the foot and cyclorama lights, and hang the cyclorama. Once again, Myers' puppet stage was standing. Next, I tried to discover how to light the shows.

Myers had constructed a lightweight aluminum lighting box with home-style rheostat dimmers. This controlled each aspect of the stage lighting (except the cyclorama lights). The box had five main dimmers, including Aux (an auxiliary used only for *Simple Simon*), Foot lights, X-Rays, Spots M (middle spots), and Spots E (end spots). The Aux, Spots M, and Spots E also had an override dimmer located on the top of the light board. I would later use the override dimmers to control Spots M and Spots E during the show. This technique allowed me to set a maximum level on the

Fig. 105. Each scene began with silhouettes in front of the brilliant blue cyclorama.

Fig. 106. Then the front lighting came on.
From "*Beauty and the Beast*"

main dimmer for a light, while using the override to quickly raise or lower the light level without making it too bright.

Each of the lights' electrical cables ran down from the light source into a harness and plugged directly into this lighting box. The lighting box then plugged into a large master dimmer which controlled the level of every light operated by the lighting box. The cyclorama lights were operated independently, and so they were wired to a separate homemade device. The control for the cyclorama lights included an on-off toggle switch attached to a home lighting dimmer. When the toggle switch was on, the cyclorama lights were at full brightness. When the switch was turned off, the lights were as bright as the dimmer had been set. This allowed for two settings of the lights during the show (a bright cyc used during scene changes and a dimmer cyc used during a scene). I continued to spend a few months learning about Myers' puppet booth and cleaning and repairing the puppets. But there was one crucial aspect not yet ready for rehearsals: the audio.

I had shipped out the audio tapes for digitalization and restoration. My rehearsal start date was determined by when the audio tapes would be digitized. There was a lot of work to be done before then. I wanted to make sure rehearsals could begin as soon as the audio tapes were ready. Besides working directly on the restoration, I also spent time searching through a box full of Myers' photos, notes, diagrams, and more. These documents provided me with a clearer understanding of how Myers had set up his shows backstage, as well as how moments in the show would look. I also used this time to become engulfed in researching Myers' career. As a trained actor, I understood the best way to accurately portray a person's art is to embrace who that person was. Not only did the research better acquaint me with Myers' unique character, but it also provided me with descriptions of his shows and visual elements which led me in the correct direction during the restaging. Needless to say, I was excited to put the bigger-than-life-sized puzzle together.

By the end of October, Myers' audiotapes were digitized and ready for rehearsal. Having seen Myers' work and remembering it well, Bart Roccoberton served as the director and advisor of the shows. I decided to rehearse *Cinderella* first, because this show had the most information to offer. Myers' notes included a diagram of where puppets would be staged at pre-show; this was a valuable resource during early rehearsals. However, the primary sources for restaging both *Cinderella* and *Beauty and the Beast* were Myers' *How-To* tapes. These tapes offered spoken stage directions from Myers himself. At times, his direction was very specific and other times it was very broad and open to interpretation.

The first rehearsal was very rough and proved I needed more time to work with the puppets and Myers' *How-To* tapes. To my unconditioned body, these puppets were very heavy and awkward. I needed to work on technical proficiency (which would develop in time). Roccoberton and I decided I should work on basic blocking and timing using the *How-To* tapes. He attended rehearsals from time to time in the early blocking stages and provided rehearsal notes. In the early rehearsals, many of my notes were about skill development, manipulation proficiency, and control, which I was still acquiring. Working every day, I listened to Myers' *How-To* tapes and started to grow more and more proficient. Though these *How-To* tapes were essential in the restaging of each show, Myers only offered the technical blocking of the show, leaving character development open for interpretation. The silent gaps Myers had left during the scenes made room for further blocking and development of character. Roccoberton would later fill in these gaps.

The control mechanisms of many of Myers' puppets are similar to each other. This enabled my skills with one puppet to transfer over to the operation of almost all of his puppets. The majority of Myers' puppets had four control centers, including two direct-rod controlled buttons and two wire-controlled levers. The lowest button (direct rod control) on the puppet's control handle allows for operation of the legs and feet of the puppet. This controller provides a direct connection to the rod-operated mechanism, which rocks right and left by twisting an internally located cam. This technique allows the legs to move alternately forward and back. The second direct control button is a rod-operated mechanism which manipulates the head. This rod is able to move right, left, up, down, and everywhere in between. The rod of the puppet goes up inside of its head where it curves around and attaches at the back. The last standard mechanisms are the two arm controls. When one of these two levers is pulled down, it tightens a wire which then causes the puppet's arm to pivot up. Although these are the standard mechanisms for most of Myers' puppets, there are also several others with more specific functions which are manipulated through unique controls.

During rehearsals for *Cinderella*, I learned about additional mechanisms Myers had used in creating and performing his puppets. A prime example of blended manipulation can be found with the Short Step-Sister from *Cinderella*. This puppet has all the standard controls as previously described. However, she also has a fifth control made with a lever and wire. When pulled, this lever pushes her tongue out of her mouth. When the lever is released, a spring returns her tongue back inside of her head. Though this puppet blends standard and unique controls, many of Myers' other puppets do not have any standard mechanisms at all. For example, the Trampoline Artist (from *Cinderella*) operates with two off-center control rods joined by a bearing. These controls enable the puppet to jump and flip in the air. Another uniquely mechanized puppet is Baby William on the piano (from *Cinderella*). This puppet is direct-rod controlled. The puppet's hands are connected to rods which extend below the play-board. The rods have two loops at the bottom, which fasten to the puppeteer's fingers. Like most of Myers' rod puppets, Baby William's head is direct-rod driven.

Though some of the puppets were easy to manipulate, a few were more of a challenge. Unlike many of Myers' puppets, the Knights have no mechanized parts. Instead, these puppets are stiff and rely solely on the puppeteer's manipulation. In order to

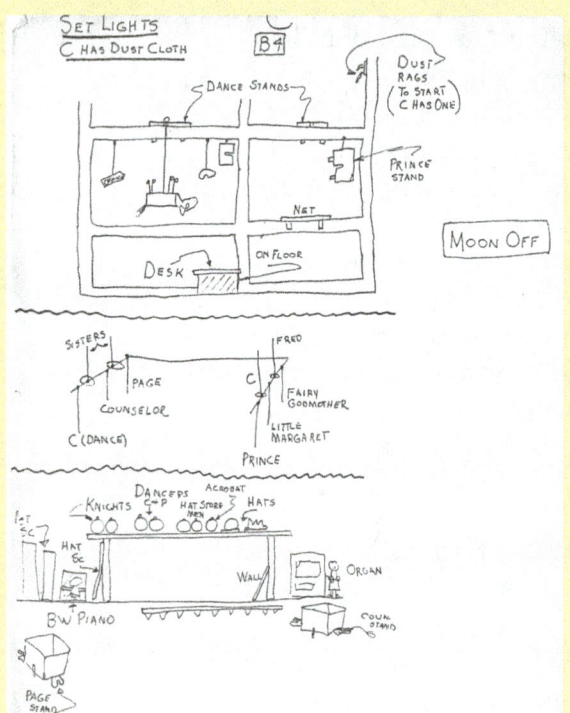

Fig. 107. Myers' preset chart for *Cinderella*.

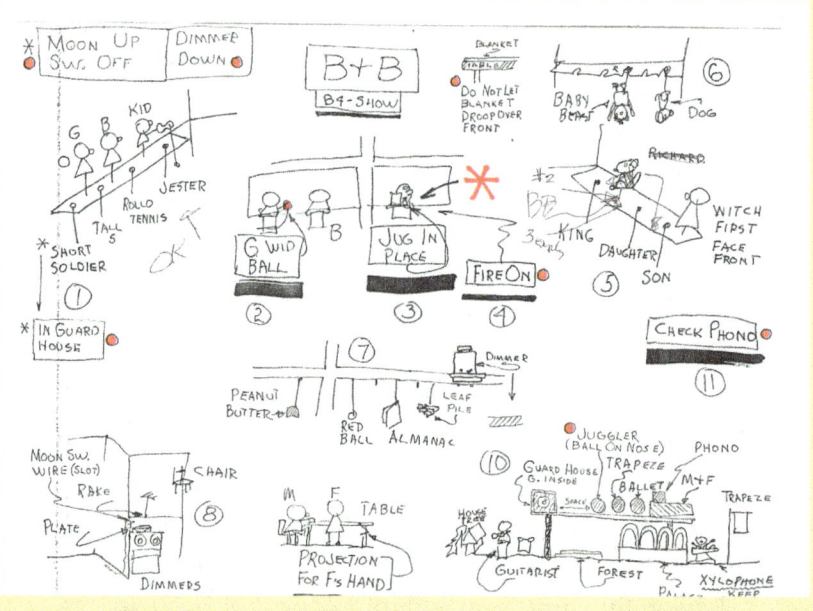

Fig. 108. Preset chart for *Beauty and the Beast*.

manipulate the Organ Grinder, I had to learn precisely how it operated. I discovered the mechanism for this puppet was operated by turning an off-center rod with one hand while playing wooden keys with another hand. The next puppets I worked with were Dancing Cinderella and Dancing Prince. Each of these puppets has direct-rods connected to its feet, moving them up and down as a button pivots on the puppet's handle. The final puppet I worked with was Little Margret. This puppet's feet are direct-rod controlled. The rods extend below the play board similarly to Baby William's on the piano. Little Margret's feet move freely, allowing her to dance a soft shoe piece.

Myers had dance experience and knowledge which he prominently featured in his puppets throughout his shows. Roccoberton and I discussed at great length the best approach to restaging dance numbers, such as the one by Little Margret. Since neither of us are dancers, the final decision was to have a trained choreographer assist with creating the dance numbers. The perfect candidate needed be someone who had strong dance skills and experience with choreography, as well as an ability to understand the limitations of a puppet. We agreed the most suitable candidate was Rachel Leigh Roccoberton Griffin.

Being the daughter of a puppeteer, Griffin had a lifetime of puppetry exposure. Additionally, she had trained as a dancer and a choreographer. She accepted the project and was ready to work. For this part of the process, I created audio files of the music for each part to be choreographed and included the *How-To* tapes for each of the scenes. Griffin studied them and then came to a later rehearsal with the dance numbers well thought out. Griffin arrived in November and over three rehearsals she was able to teach me the major dance numbers of *Cinderella*. These included *Fred and Cinderella Dance*, *The Knight's Battle*, *The Royal Dance of the Kingdom*, and *The Little Margret Dance*. Sometimes the choreography offered was physically difficult and worked muscles I had not previously used during rehearsals. Ultimately, the dance numbers were achieved and moved with fluidity.

Fig. 109 and 110. Demonstrating a scene without stage masking.

Once these numbers were choreographed, it was up to me to continue to rehearse and build up my strength and endurance. From late October until late February, Roccoberton and I continued to shape Myers' *Cinderella* into a stronger and stronger show. When not rehearsing *Cinderella*, I spent my time designing and curating the Dick Myers museum exhibit (detailed in Chapter 6). With the opening date of the performance coming up, I knew it was time to begin working on *Beauty and the Beast*.

When I started rehearsals for *Beauty and the Beast*, I found the process to be much easier. By this time, my body was more prepared for the physical demands of a Myers show. Unlike *Cinderella*, *Beauty and the Beast* did not have a written script with scenic drawings. However, Myers did have a formula which worked for his scripts. Thus, the mental work that went into restaging this show was immensely lessened due to already having staged *Cinderella*. While rehearsing *Beauty and the Beast*, I found the scene transitions were much simpler than those in *Cinderella*, though this did not make *Beauty and the Beast* any less complicated overall. The differences between the two shows were their different types of complexity. At the beginning of Myers' career, he created his puppet shows with rich storylines as in *Cinderella*. However, in later shows (such as *Beauty and the Beast*) he replaced deep storylines and character development with complex puppetry entertainment. *Beauty and the Beast* had many complex and challenging puppets and moments to restage.

As in *Cinderella*, many of the puppets in *Beauty and the Beast* were constructed with traditional Myers' mechanics. Also as in *Cinderella*, there were several exceptions to this. The first puppet I explored was the Juggler. This puppet is fairly rigid in construction, with a direct rod-controlled arm. The performance capabilities of this puppet include the ability to spin plates on a stick, balance a ball on his nose, and balance a chair on a stick. The next puppet I worked with was the Guitar Player. This puppet is very complex in construction, but the slightest movements create a truly poetic performance. The puppet is on a pedestal and has a rod-con-

trolled hand which strums the guitar. With the movements of the rod-controlled head, not only can the puppet's body sway, but the puppet's other hand will move up and down along the fret board of the guitar. Another interesting set of puppets included the sitting versions of Geraldine and the Beast. Sitting Geraldine's feet can rock back and forth by a direct rod control mechanism attached to a cam. Whereas, Dancing Geraldine has direct rod-controlled feet and a rod control to push the arms up or pull them down.

The most difficult of all these puppets was the Trapeze Artist. This puppet is completely separate from the trapeze, but has small hooks on its hands to catch onto it. During the act, the puppet transitions from standing to sitting and to hanging on the trapeze, all while the trapeze is still swinging. While hanging from the trapeze, the puppet lets go, spins in a 360-degree turn, and then once again grabs ahold of the trapeze.

Finally, Baby William and the xylophone was another very complex and time-consuming puppet. Myers designed the xylophone backwards. Nevertheless, this version of Baby William operates much like the piano player in *Cinderella*.

Just as with *Cinderella*, I first allowed Myers' audio tapes to coach me through *Beauty and the Beast*. By the time I invited Roccoberton to give his direction, it was already an entertaining, albeit unpolished, production. In fact, the first run-through of the show kept Roccoberton laughing throughout the entire performance. However, there was much work to be done. Roccoberton advised me through the show, helping to find some truly wonderful moments. Together we found one lovely, yet dark and humorous moment when melodramatic music played from the old record player as Beast was being kicked out of his parents' house.

Myers strongly incorporated dance into *Beauty and the Beast,* as in *Cinderella,* and Griffin was invited back to choreograph the dance numbers. Although *Beauty and the Beast* did not have as many dance numbers as *Cinderella,* it still had a number of complicated pieces. The first piece needing choreography was the waltz which the Beast and Geraldine share as their friendship develops. The second most complex dance needing choreography was the ballet at the closing of the show. This ballet featured Geraldine jumping and spinning all around the stage. Griffin (while seven months pregnant) again brought fully-realized dance numbers with exciting choreography that was appropriate and seemingly close to Myers' original staging.

There was, however, a moment during the Witch's dance where Myers stated in his *How-To* tape, "she does a backward thing right here." Clueless as to what he meant, we (Roccoberton, Griffin, and I) obtained permission from Alleu Kurten to adapt a dance as we felt was fitting: a rendition of the moonwalk. For Myers, the backwards dancing note to self on his *How-To* tapes may have been connected back to his study of dance and the mime walking in the wind movement best know performed by Marcel Marceau and Étienne Decroux. Once the choreography was set, I continued to rehearse, perfecting the show day by day.

When *Beauty and the Beast* had become a strong show, I transitioned back to rehearsing *Cinderella.* Through staging *Beauty and the Beast,* I had learned much more about Myers' puppetry style and his sense of humor, and I was then able to apply these insights to the work I was doing on *Cinderella.* This helped me discover humor in moments which had previously seemed serious.

After two additional weeks rehearsing *Cinderella,* I started to rehearse the shows back to back. Although I would have an assistant during the run for the Connecticut Repertory Theatre, she was not yet available. Therefore, I made the transition between the shows on my own. I set up two tables and spread out all the puppets, sets, and props for *Beauty and the Beast*. *Cinderella* was set for preshow in Myers' puppet booth. Once a run of *Cinderella* was finished, I would set a timer for fifteen minutes on my phone and efficiently transition between the two shows. As the *Cinderella* puppets were transferred to the tables, I would also be preparing puppets from *Beauty and the Beast* in the puppet booth. My first attempt at this was completed in just over twelve minutes. For the performances at the Connecticut Repertory Theatre, my transitions assistant, Xing Xin Liu, would help drastically reduce this time. When my fifteen minute timer went off, it was time to start a rehearsal of *Beauty and the Beast*.

During the next two weeks, I rehearsed in this manner every day. Sometimes I would take a half hour break after running both shows, then reset and rehearse the shows again. I discovered an eight-hour rehearsal was a little much on my body. Therefore, I would often take an hour or more break between double runs. Every day, it seemed my proficiency with the puppets increased, and the shows seemed to be easier and easier to perform. Roccoberton was still actively attending rehearsals and offering productive notes and insight on the shows.

During the week leading up to the show, Roccoberton approached me with a concern. He told me it appeared as if Baby William was playing the xylophone backwards. I had not thought about this before. However, Roccoberton was right. Myers had built the xylophone backwards. Although I could see the size of the different keys on the xylophone, the audience could not, so from their perspective they might perceive Baby William was playing backwards. To correct their perception, I had to pretend the xylophone was built the correct way. This meant playing the low notes on the smallest keys and the high notes on the largest keys. I had very little time to rehearse this change before moving the shows into the Studio Theatre.

On April 9, 2013, Roccoberton, Paul Spirito, and I loaded the shows into the Studio Theatre at the University of Connecticut.

That evening, we began the first dress rehearsal for the show. Performing in the Studio Theatre offered many new challenges. I soon discovered that, even though I had room to spread out, the table used to hold some of the puppets needed to be very close to the puppet booth to ensure the transitions between set pieces and puppets were quick, smooth, and efficient. I also discovered that, during the show, my only light source would come from the lights from the puppet booth. At first this was little disorienting, but I soon adapted. At this point, Liu had joined my process and offered assistance during the quick change-over between shows.

The shows were performed at the Studio Theatre on April 12-14, 2013. Overall, the opening performance was successful and did not have too many problems. However, the opening was not flawless. Prior to the performance, I turned the puppet stage lights on and they quickly went out. One of the fuses burned out and needed to be changed. Luckily, there was a container of new fuses taped to the lighting board. Thank you, Dick Myers! The next mishap occurred in the scene where the Tall Sister tries on the shoe. Suddenly, the Tall Sister's foot fell off right before the Prince asked her to sit down and try on the shoe. Luckily, the audience did not notice this flaw, but backstage it seemed like a major catastrophe. After the intermission, I performed *Beauty and the Beast* when another disaster struck: one of the Guard's arm wires snapped. This made the arm inoperable for the performance. Overall, though, the opening performance was well received and had an excellent audience turnout. The following day I repaired both puppets.

On the 13th, the shows again had a few technical difficulties behind the scenes. While setting up for the evening's performances, Liu approached me with the Juggler (from *Beauty and the Beast*); a hand had broken off of the puppet. A thin rope had joined the arm and the hand together with a flexible joint which had held the hand together. I quickly repaired the broken rope before the shows started. This repair required drilling out the old rope and replacing it with some new rope from my repair kit. The shows on

the 13th were successful. However, I was a little nervous about the next day's performance.

The performance on the 14th was viewed by nearly the entire Connecticut Guild of Puppetry. The guild had graciously decided to attend both the Dick Myers museum exhibit and the Dick Myers Project shows. Many of the older members of the guild remember Myers' work fondly and were excited to once again see a performance of it. Larry Engler, having attended the show on the 12th, asked to view this performance from backstage. It was a request that I found puzzling at first. I wondered why anyone would want to see a sweaty puppeteer in action. After later watching a video of my backstage performance, I understood the appeal of watching a puppeteer "dance" during a show. My own physicality and choreography backstage goes unnoticed by the audience during a show. This leaves the audience unaware of how physically involved I am during the entire show. I am always moving in order for the story to run smoothly and flawlessly. Their only chance at insight comes at the end of each show, when I offer the audience a glimpse into my backstage world, as Myers had done, by performing a scene with the curtain dropped, exposing the puppeteer and the puppets' mechanisms to the entire audience.

Once the shows had been completed for the Connecticut Repertory Theatre, I continued to rehearse and refine my performance. During the summer of 2013, I performed both shows several more times. The next performance was arranged because Caroll Spinney (Big Bird and Oscar the Grouch) requested it. Spinney had contacted Roccoberton to inquire about the next public performance. However, there had not yet been any additional performances planned so Roccoberton and I agreed a performance should be arranged for Spinney and it would be opened to the public. When he arrived, I performed *Beauty and the Beast* for him, his wife Debra Spinney, and a small audience. After the show, I had a talk back with Spinney, during which he and I discussed his memories of Myers as well as Spinney's career to date. After a few minutes of the talk back, Spinney pulled out a duffle bag and revealed that

Fig. 111. Oscar the Grouch with Caroll Spinney critique Seth's performance.

inside was Oscar the Grouch. Oscar critiqued the show in a hilarious banter that had the audience and myself laughing.

Once the audience had left, we went to lunch and continued the conversation we had started in front of the audience. I learned a lot about Myers' work in puppetry and television. I left lunch early in order to set up for a performance of *Cinderella*. Once again, after the show Spinney and I did a talk back during which Oscar the Grouch made an appearance which delighted the audience. Since Myers built the shows for puppeteers, I was excited and grateful to see Spinney's reactions to this revival. I hoped to hear the thoughts of many additional puppeteers.

I wanted to bring *Beauty and the Beast* to a puppet community. One of the best places to present puppet works to young and old puppeteers is at the National Puppetry Conference at the Eugene O'Neil Theater Center in Waterford, Connecticut. This is an intensive conference offered every year where workshops are offered and puppeteers can come together to make great art. Each season is kicked off by professional performances, and I was granted the honor of performing Myers' *Beauty and the Beast* on June 9th, 2013,

Fig. 112. Post performance inspection of the Witch's potion machine from "*Beauty and the Beast*".

Fig. 113. Question and Answer session following Seth's performance.

immediately after Philip Huber performed his amazing marionettes. The experience was wonderful. This performance truly provided me with an understanding of how timeless the piece was. For the first time in several decades, *Beauty and the Beast* was performed for its intended audience.

During the summer of 2013, the Ballard Institute and Museum of Puppetry offered a summer series presenting public performances by students in the Puppet Arts Program at the University of Connecticut. On July 6, 2013, I performed *Cinderella* and followed up this performance with a production of *Beauty and the Beast* on July 20, 2013. Both performances were very well received. This performance was my last production of *Beauty and the Beast*. Soon after, I packed up the puppets in Myers' touring boxes. I had one final performance as part of my MFA project: the Puppet Festival (R)Evolution (the 75th National Puppetry Festival), where I performed *Cinderella* to an audience entirely composed of puppeteers.

The performance at the Festival (R)Evolution was one of the most nerve-wracking moments of my project, but also gave me the deepest appreciation for what it might have felt like to be Dick Myers. This performance of *Cinderella* was held on August 9, 2013, at 8:00 P.M. It was placed in a prime position – the Friday evening performance. I had heard there was much anticipation among puppeteers in attendance. During the weeklong festival, I grew more and more nervous because I couldn't rehearse the show for over a week prior to this performance. On the 9th, I finally had a chance to rehearse the show in the space. The rehearsal went very well, which boosted my confidence for the evening performance. I spent the day keeping myself calm and collected and did not attend workshops or performances. In the evening, the performance of *Cinderella* was one of the best performances I had done to date. Once the evening show was over, I felt an overwhelming appreciation for Myers' work and career. I understood how Myers' must have felt after a performance for his peers. As in every other performance, I offered the audience a chance to view the show from

back stage. I dropped the puppet booth curtain, and performed the scene with Cinderella and the Fairy Godmother. After the show, the audience was invited on stage to briefly look behind the scenes to see how the backstage was organized. The show seemed to be well received by the older puppeteers who remember Myers' work fondly. Additionally, the show was a success among the younger generations who had never seen Myers' work. I believe this performance aided in creating a conversation among the elder puppeteers and the young generation of puppeteers. This performance justified the intensive year and a half I spent researching, restoring, and remounting the shows.

8

Project Review

When I started working on The Dick Myers Project, I set high expectations and goals for myself and the outcome of the project. The first goal of this project was to restore and preserve Myers' puppets. Secondly, to create a documentary honoring the life and works of Myers. Finally, to remount, perform, and document Myers' shows. Through each part of the process, I found myself enriched by the multifaceted aspects of this project. This pursuit aided in my continual growth and knowledge in puppet construction, puppet history, and performance.

I discovered many puppet building techniques and repairs which I had not known before, such as creating handmade rope, working with Plastic Wood, and creating cardboard and muslin pop-up set pieces, to name a few. Many, if not all, of the puppet building techniques I came to acquire have and will continue to influence my work as a puppeteer and in other art forms. Through my research during this part of the process, I found a few techniques which Myers had used and was able to apply them. By gaining a strong understanding of Myers' building techniques, I was able to understand the puppet and its performance possibilities.

However, I knew in order to more strongly connect with the puppets, I needed to understand the puppeteer who had created them.

Much of the success of this project can be attributed to researching Myers' life and his work. The more I learned about his past and who he was, the better I understood his puppetry. Although I did research throughout this entire project, the research was not organized into a comprehensive timeline until I was asked by Dr. John Bell to serve as the curator for the museum exhibit on Myers' life. Suddenly, I needed to make sure all of my acquired facts were precisely correct. At first, this proved to be a challenge. Much of my information about Myers had been shared from the memories of those who had known him. Therefore, in some cases, the memories about Myers were varied, but overall, I was able to combine the information I had received. With these rich facts and stories, a cohesive exhibit was created about his life and works.

Through many interviews, I gained personal insight about not only Myers' life and work in puppetry, but also about the puppeteers I had interviewed. By talking with puppeteers such as Allelu Kurten and Luman Coad, I came to understand the ways in which they also had shaped the world of puppetry. These discussions alone proved to be invaluable information that one could not simply access through a textbook. To supplement the exhibit, I also created a dedication video about Myers, and when I completed both the dedication video and the museum exhibit on Myers, I had felt each had further influenced not only my understanding of his work, but also the way in which I rehearsed and performed his shows.

As a performer, I believe in the idea of function over form. This means I have higher expectations for what a puppet can do than how pretty it looks. Nevertheless, part of my intention upon arriving at the University of Connecticut was to learn how to create work which was both practical and aesthetically beautiful. Through Myers' puppetry, I learned even the simplest creations can become beautiful if constructed well and performed in the right hands. These two notions carried over into my rehearsals. Throughout the rehearsal process, I seldom allowed myself the opportunity to think the show was shaped as beautifully as it truly would become. I was always searching for ways to improve my manipulation skills, allowing the show to flow smoothly with apparently little effort from myself.

Upon the arrival of my first performance for an audience, I realized the dedication had paid off. When performing *Cinderella* and *Beauty and the Beast*, I was engulfed by the two stories and felt the puppets in essence were an extension of me. Although I was proud of my performances, I was anxious to hear the thoughts of all generations of puppeteers. Was Dick Myers' work as valuable today as it had been forty years ago? Performing *Cinderella* at the 75th National Puppetry Festival provided the answer to this question. At the National Puppetry Festival, I was honored with the Fan Favorite Award, which was voted upon by all participants at the festival. Myers' shows are timeless. Many of the comments I received from audience members indicated surprise there was only one puppeteer performing the entire show. Although there were not many reviews written about my performances, what I heard from the audience members after each show was rather delightful. Audience members were captivated by Myers' unique puppets and storytelling. For many, the show felt like an "old fashioned puppet show": the stories are as timeless as when they were conceived. The remounting of Myers' shows was a success.

A revival of this magnitude has never happened before in puppetry. Any hidden doubts I had about the success of the project were alleviated by Allelu Kurten. After seeing the performance of *Cinderella* and *Beauty and the* Beast, she bestowed upon me the best review to date. "His voices were heard. His puppets performed with ease and smooth manipulation. The lights came up and I was expecting Dick Myers to appear…and then Seth stepped out from behind the curtain. I was surprised and happy."

Fig. 114. Dick Myers after his performance at the UNIMA Congress in Charleville-Mezierres, France in 1972.

9 Scripts

Dick Whittington and His Cat

(a synopsis)

This is the story of a country boy who walks to London where he believes the streets are paved with gold. The story concerns itself with Dick's trip to London and his adventures after arriving.

Scene 1 – THE FARM: On his way to London Dick meets a farmer who gives him a cat.

Scene 2 – THE TRAVELER: Dick and his cat meet a traveler and his duck.

Scene 3 – A STREET IN LONDON: Dick and the cat find the London streets are not paved with gold. Dick meets Alice, the Sea Captain's daughter; the mean old housekeeper; and the good Sea Captain who lets Dick and his cat come and live in his house.

Scene 4 – THE KITCHEN: Dick washes dishes for the housekeeper.

Scene 5 – THE ATTIC: a pantomime scene.

Scene 6 – THE FAREWELL: It is the custom whenever the Captain goes on a voyage, everyone in the household must give him something to take along and trade. Dick has nothing but his cat and so the Captain takes Dick's cat and sails away.

Scene 7 – THE VOYAGE TO A DISTANT KINGDOM

Scene 8 – THE PALACE: Here the Captain is entertained by the King's Magician. Dick's cat rids the palace of mice and the King gives the Captain a bag of gold.

Scene 9 - THE RETURN VOYAGE

Scene 10 – HAPPY ENDING

Scene 1 – THE FARM

Introduction music

Narrator: Once upon a time there was a little boy named Dick Whittington.

Music - Dick appears - walks across the stage and disappears.

Narrator: And there was a very special cat.

Music - cat appears

Narrator: One day the little boy passed by.

Music - Dick reenters

Dick: Hello.

Farmer: Hello little boy. What are you doing way out here in the country?

Dick: My name is Dick Whittington and I'm on my way to London.

Farmer: London is a long way off. What are you going to do there?

Dick: People say in London all the streets are paved with gold. Everyone is rich and you can play all day long.

Farmer: You know, I've heard that too. Just think, streets paved with gold.

Dick: Yes, and all you need do is pick up some gold and you're rich – but London is so far and I get so lonely walking by myself.

Farmer: How would you like a cat to take with you, then you wouldn't be so lonely.

Dick: Oh, I'd like that.

Farmer: Well here's a nice kitty. I have so many cats on my farm that I'd hardly miss this one – Kitty, would you like to go to London with Dick?

Cat: meow

Farmer: Well then it's settled. You take good care of the kitty, Dick.

Dick: I will. Oh we'll have lots of fun together.

Farmer: Well, you come back and see me now when you get all the gold you want.

Dick: I will and thank you very much for the kitty.

Farmer: That's alright. Good bye.

Dick: Bye, bye. Come on kitty.

Nar: And so off they went, Dick and the cat. Off toward the great city of London.

Music up - lights down - Dick and cat exit - setup next scene.

Scene 2 – THE TRAVELER

Traveler enters with box on his back. Then Dick enters (both to music).

Dick: Hello.

Traveler: Hello.

Dick: My name is Dick Whittington and this is my cat. We're on our way to London.

Traveler: London. That's still pretty far away.

Dick: I'm very thirsty. Do you know where I can get a drink of water?

Traveler: Well yes I do. There's a stream of water close by.

Narrator: The traveler put down the box he was carrying and he and Dick went to look for a drink of water.

Dick and Traveler exit.
A duck comes out of the box and the cat chases it.
(Music) Traveler and Dick enter

Dick: Thank you, I feel much much better. Oh, where's my Kitty? Here kitty kitty kitty. Here kitty kitty.

Cat enters

Dick: Oh .. here kitty.

Traveler: London is off in that direction. I hope you arrive safely.

Dick: Thank you very much and bye bye. Come on kitty.

Cat: meow

Lights down - music up - scene change

Scene 3 – A STREET IN LONDON

Enter a baker with a stack of bread. He knocks on door and housekeeper comes out.

Housekeeper: Well what do you want, what do you want, no no we don't want any, we don't want any, go away, go away!

She pushes the baker and he falls, spilling all the bread. Housekeeper exits into house.

Music - Dick and cat enter and stand downstage.

Narrator: When Dick and the cat arrived in London they found it very different from what they had imagined. The streets weren't pave with gold, they were just plain streets.

Dick: Kitty I think we've looked on every street in London and still no gold. I'm tired and hungry.

Cat: meow

Enter Housekeeper

Housekeeper: Well, what are you doing around here. We don't like little boys around here. Go away, go away, go away!

Exit Housekeeper

Music - enter Alice (Captain's daughter)

Alice: Hello.

Dick: Hello. I'm Dick Whittington and this is my cat.

Alice: My name is Alice and I've just come from my singing lesson. Would you like to hear me sing?

Dick: Oh yes.

Alice: (*sings*) Mary had a little lamb, little lamb, little lamb. Mary had a little lamb, its fleece was white as snow. And everywhere that Mary went, Mary went, Mary went. Everywhere that Mary went the lamb was sure to go.

Dick: That was very nice. Thank you.

Alice: I must go home now or the housekeeper will scold me. She's very old and mean. Bye bye.

Dick: Bye bye. Wasn't she a pretty girl?

Cat: meow

Music - enter Sea Captain

Capt: Hello. What are you doing in front of my house?

Dick: My name is Dick Whittington and this is my cat. We walked all the way to London to see the streets paved with gold.

Capt: But there aren't any.

Dick: We found that out. And now we're cold and hungry and no place to sleep.

Capt: I'm very sorry for you Dick but I'm afraid I can't help you. I must hurry along now or the housekeeper will be mad with me. Good bye. Oh wait one moment. I just thought of something. My housekeeper is always complaining that I give her too much work to do and my daughter Alice has no mother and is very lonely. I was just thinking, if you want to come and work for the housekeeper and be company for my daughter, then you and your cat can come and live in my house. How would you like that?

Dick: Oh yes.

Cat: meow

Capt: Well then you come along with me.

Dick: Oh thank you. Come on kitty.

Music up - lights down - change scene

Scene 4 – THE KITCHEN

Dick is onstage as the lights come up.

Narrator: So it was that Dick and the cat came to live with the good Sea Captain and his daughter and the mean old housekeeper.

Enter housekeeper.

Housekeeper: Dick Whittington here are some more dishes for you to wash.

Dick washes dishes. Breaks one.

Housekeeper: What happened, what happened, what happened? Oh you clumsy boy.

Housekeeper exits. Alice enters.

Alice: Hello Dick.

Dick: Hello Alice.

Alice: Is the housekeeper making you do the dishes again?

Dick: Yes and I'm so tired. All I do is work for her.

Alice: I came down to see if you would dance with me.

Dick: Well I don't dance very well but I'll try.

Alice: All right then. You just follow me.

*Music - Dick and Alice dance.
At end of dance Alice exits. Enter Housekeeper.*

Housekeeper: Dick Whittington here are some more dishes for you to wash.

Dick washes dishes and lights go down - music up -- set next scene.

Scene 5 – THE ATTIC

*This is a pantomime scene where Dick is forced to sleep in the attic.
The mice keep Dick awake until the cat chases them away.*

Scene 6 – THE FAREWELL

Narrator: At last the day came when the Captain was to leave on a long ocean voyage to a far distant kingdom. It was the custom that everyone in the household would give the Captain something to take along and trade.

Empty stage - enter Captain (music)

Capt: Dick. Dick Whittington!

Enter Dick

Dick: Yes Captain.

Capt: What are you going to give me to take along on the voyage?

Dick: I'm sorry, Captain. I don't have a thing.

Capt: But Dick everyone else has given me something.

Dick: I'm sorry but I just don't have anything.

Enter cat.

Cat: meow meow

Capt: I know. I'll take your kitty.

Dick: Oh no. If you take my kitty, the mouse won't let me sleep at night and I'll miss him so.

Capt: But Dick, everyone must give me something to trade.

Dick: Well all right then. You may take my kitty.

Capt: Thank you very much, Dick. Good bye.

Dick: Bye bye.

Dick and cat have a bit of pantomime.

Scene 7 – VOYAGE TO FAR DISTANT KINGDOM

A pantomime scene of small boat sailing across the stage (music)

Scene 8 – THE PALACE

King is onstage as lights go up. Enter Page (to music)

Page: Hey King! There's a visitor to see you.

King: Well show him in.

Page: Alright King.

Page exits. Captain and Page enter. They do a short dance.

Page: King meet the Sea Captain. Sea Captain meet the King.

Capt: Your Majesty.

King: Welcome to our country, Captain. We have been expecting you. Page announce the entertainment.

Page: Ya, King. Announcing the world's most famous magician who will do some magic for us.

Magician enters and does his tricks:
(1) bouncing balls (2) bubbles (3) single flower (4) bunch of flowers.
Exit Magician.

King: Let us eat. Page go get the food.

Page: Ya, King.

Page exits and returns with food. Mice appear and take away food.

King: We have a terrible time here, Captain.

Page: Ya, terrible.

King: Our country is overrun with these little animals and they eat all our food.

Page: Ya, all our food.

King: Page, go bring us some more food.

Page: Ya, sure King.

Page exits and returns with food. Mice appear and take away food.

King: You see. I don't know what we're going to do. We've tried everything in our power to get rid of them but nothing works.

Capt: Your Majesty have you thought of keeping a cat.

Page: Ya, a cat.

King: What is a cat?

Page: Ya, what's a cat?

Capt: Your Majesty, a cat is a little animal that catches mice.

King: Oh if we only had such an animal here in this country.

Page: Ya.

King: Quiet, Page!

Capt: It just so happens, your Majesty, that I do have a cat. With your permission I'll call him. Here kitty kitty. Here kitty kitty.

Enter cat

Cat: meow

Capt: Now watch this.

Page exits and returns with food. Mice appear but are frightened off by cat.

King: Wonderful! Wonderful! Wonderful! Page go fetch a bag of gold for the Captain.

Page: Ya, King

Page exits and returns with bag of gold.

King: Captain you have done us a great service. We are forever indebted to you for ridding our country of those little animals you call mice.

Capt: Thank you, your Majesty.

Page: Ya thank you.

Capt: Your Majesty it was a pleasure to serve you.

Music up - lights dim - set next scene

Scene 9 – RETURN VOYAGE

This is a reverse of Scene 7. Boat travels in opposite direction.

Scene 10 – HAPPY ENDING

Takes place in Kitchen.

Housekeeper: Dick Whittington. Dick Whittington, come here.

Enter Dick

Dick: Yes.

Housekeeper: What have you been doing? There's dishes to be done, dishes to be washed, here they are, do the dishes.

Dick: Oh alright.

Enter Alice (Dick doesn't wash the dishes)

Dick: Hello Alice.

Alice: Hello.

Dick: It has been a long time since the Captain went away and I miss my kitty. I guess I'd better get started on these dishes before that old housekeeper comes back. She scolds me all the time. Listen! Listen, it sounds like the kitty Oh it is. It is, it is. Here kitty here kitty.

Enter cat and Captain

Dick: (*to cat*) Oh am I glad to see you.

Capt: Hello Dick, hello Alice.

Dick: You didn't trade my kitty after all.

Capt: No indeed. And I have a most wonderful surprise for you. Your kitty chased all the mice for the King and in return he gave me a bag of gold for you. It's all yours. Come along Alice, I've many things to tell you.

Exit Captain and Alice. Enter Housekeeper.

Housekeeper: Well Dick Whittington why aren't you doing the dishes? Why aren't you doing the dishes?

Dick: Poo! I'll never have to do the dishes again. So there, so there, so there.

Dick knocks the dishes on the floor with a crash.

Housekeeper: Well I never!

Exit Housekeeper.

Dick: Just think kitty, we have the gold after all. We're rich, we're rich, we're rich!

Music up - Dick and cat do dance.

Narrator: So it was that Dick never again had to do the dishes and when he grew up he became Lord Mayor of London and he and the Captain's daughter were married and they all lived happily ever after.

Music up

Cinderella

(a synopsis)

Scene 1 – STEP-SISTERS' HOUSE: Cinderella and her best friend, a mouse named Fred, dust the house. The step-sisters leave for the Hat Store to buy new hats because they are invited to the Prince's Ball. Cinderella has not been invited to the Ball.

Scene 2 – THE PRINCE'S OFFICE: the Prince and his Counselor talk about the forthcoming Ball and how the Prince is to dance with the girl chosen to be The Most Beautiful Girl at the Ball. The Prince and the Counselor tne audition two entertainers for the Ball: first an acrobat and secondly a pianist.

Scene 3 – THE HAT STORE: the Step-sisters buy two old hats that are about to be thrown out.

Scene 4 – AT HOME: the sisters leave for the Ball and Cinderella meets her Fairy Godmother. The Fairy Godmother changes Cinderella's old clothes into a beautiful new dress and changes Fred into a horse for Cinderella to ride to the Ball. The Fairy Godmother warns Cinderella not to stay out after 12 o'clock because after midnight both Cinderella's new clothes and Fred will change back as they were before.

Scene 5 – THE BALL: first we are entertained by two Knights who do a battle for us. Then a musician plays for us. Next the Prince dances with The Most Beautiful Girl at the Ball (who turns out to be Cinderella). After the dance the Prince asks Cinderella to tell her name but before she can tell us, the clock strikes 12 and Cinderella runs off.

Scene 6 – OUTSIDE THE PALACE WALL: Cinderella is back in her old dress and Fred is a mouse again. The Prince and the Counselor do not recognize Cinderella. The Prince finds one of Cinderella's shoes.

Scene 7 – OFFICE: the Counselor tries to cheer up the Prince by having Little Margaret dance for him. The Counselor makes the suggestion that they try the Most Beautiful Girl's shoe on every girl in the Kingdom and when they find the girl it fits then they will have found The Most Beautiful Girl.

Scene 8 – HOME AGAIN: trying on of the shoe.

Scene 1 – STEP-SISTERS' HOUSE

Introduction Music

Narrator: Once upon a time there was a girl named Cinderella.

Music- enter Cinder who begins dusting the house.

Music - enter Fred (the mouse).

Cinder: Hello Fred. Fred would you like to help me dust?

Fred shakes head no!

Cinder: But you would if I asked you nicely, wouldn't you? Wouldn't you?

Fred nods yes.

Cinder: Go get a dust cloth.

Fred goes into closet and returns with dust cloth, starts to dust and then begins to dance to music.

Cinder: *(over music)* Fred, please don't start to dance. If you start to dance then I'll start to dance and then I'll never get the dusting done. Oh well.

Both Fred and Cinder dance.

Tall Sister: (*from off stage*) Cinderella!

Narrator: Cinderella lived with her two step-sisters.

Tall Sister: Cinderella!

Cinder: Bye Fred. Don't forget to put the dust cloth away.

Fred exits into closet. Enter Tall Sister (at top of stairs)

Tall Sister: Cinderella! Your sister and I are coming down.

Tall Sister comes down the stairs.

Tall Sister: Have you finished dusting?

Cinder: Almost.

Tall Sister: Well hurry up, there's others things to be done. Your sister and I are going to the Hat Store and buy some new hats. We're invited to the Prince's Ball. Hurry up sister or we'll be late.

Short Sister comes down stairs.

Tall Sister: Cinderella, after you have finished dusting, do the dishes, cut the grass, and carry out the garbage. By that time you sister and I will be back from the Hat Store.

Cinder: I wish I could go to the Prince's Ball.

Tall Sister: You can't go. Only the important members of the family are invited. Besides, no one likes you.

Short Sister: Sister, tell Cinderella she can't go to the Prince's Ball.

Tall Sister: I just told her she couldn't go. Don't you ever listen to anything?

Short Sister: I know why Cinderella wants to go to the Ball. Because she's in love with the Prince.

Tall Sister: Your sister says you want to go to the Prince's Ball because you're in love with the Prince. Is that true?

Short Sister: Look at the back of the cupboard door, you'll see.

Cinder: No!

*Tall Sister looks behind the cupboard door and
finds a picture of the Prince.
Cinderella has pinned the picture there.*

Tall Sister: A picture of the Prince. Ha! Ha!

Cinder: It's not funny.

Tall Sister: Just remember, Cinderella, it is better to have loved and lost than never to have lived in a glass house.

Short Sister: That's wrong. It should be –

Tall Sister: Shut up!!

Short Sister sticks out tongue.

Tall Sister: Your sister and I are going to the Hat Store now. We'll be the best looking girls at the Ball. Come on!

Sisters exit to music. Cinder goes to closet.

Cinder: It's alright Fred, you can come out.

Fred comes out of closet.

Cinder: You're the best friend I have, you know that Fred?

Fred nods head yes and Fred and Cinder dance till end of scene.

Music change - scene change.

Scene 2 – THE PRINCE'S OFFICE

Prince is sitting at desk.

Prince: Page!

Page enters

Prince: Page find the Counselor and tell him I want to see him.

Exit Page.

Prince: It's almost time for the Ball and I must see how the plans are progressing.

Music - enter Counselor.

Counsel: You wanted to see me, Prince?

Prince: Yes, Counselor I would like to know how the plans are coming along for the Ball. Has everyone in the Kingdom been invited?

Counsel: Yes Prince, everyone that we know of. And don't forget, Prince, that you are to dance with the most beautiful girl at the Ball.

Prince: I won't forget, that's fun.

Counsel: And also Prince, remember that you're a grown man now and you must soon be getting married. So be sure and look at all the girls at the Ball.

Prince: I will. And the entertainment, how's the entertainment coming?

Counsel: It just so happens, Prince, that I'm going to audition several people right now. Would you like to watch?

Prince: Yes I would.

Counsel: Very well. The first will be an acrobat who will perform for us.

Acrobat enters and does his act and exits.

Prince: He was good. Is there any more?

Counsel: Yes, Baby William is going to play the piano. Is Baby William ready? Alright send him up.

Baby William plays piano and exits.

Counsel: Thank you, Baby William.

Prince: I like him. Well, it looks like it's going to be a great Ball this year ..I can hardly wait! Remember last year those two ugly sisters came and wore those awful hats.

Counsel: Yes, I remember, Prince. I remember.

Music up - lights down - set next scene.

Scene 3 – THE HAT SHOP

Enter Short Hat Man

SHM: Alfredo .. Alfredo!

Enter Tall Hat Man

SHM: Alfredo, what are we going to do with these hats, they're monstrous!!

THM: They're hideous!

SHM: They're awful!

THM: They're insidious.

SHM: Should we throw them out? Surely no one would want these.

THM: But wait, but wait! You never can tell.

Entrance bell rings.

SHM: Quick! It's those awful sisters. Maybe we will sell these hats at last.

THM: Maybe at last we will sell these hats.

Music - enter sisters.

Tall Sister: We've come to look at some hats. We're going to the Prince's Ball.

SHM: Well then, madam, you've come to the right place. You are in luck for we have just received two of the most beautiful hats we've ever had.

Tall Sister: Wonderful. Show them to us.

SHM: Here they are, madam. Look at these.

Tall Sister: Beautiful! Beautiful! How can I lose with a hat like this?

SHM: Lose?

Tall Sister: Yes, at the Prince's Ball. I'm sure to be chosen most beautiful of all. We'll try the hats on now. I'll go first, sister.

Tall Sister exits and returns with hat on head (music)

Tall Sister: Oh, it fits just fine.

SHM: Beautiful.

THM: It's gorgeous.

Short Sister sticks out tongue.

Short Sister: I'll try the other one on now.

Short Sister exits and returns with hat on head.

SHM: Wonderful.

THM: It's stunning!

Tall Sister: Ugh! We'll take them. Come on sister let's go.

Sisters exit to music.

SHM: Hats – hats - hats. We make them.

THM: And we mend them.

SHM: And we buy them.

THM: And we sell them.

SHM: But really, isn't it awful? Why do they wear them?

THM: What can it be?

SHM: Oh well, it make us rich.

THM: And it makes them happy.

SHM: Isn't it awful.

THM: Isn't it horrid.

Both exit to music - lights dim - scene change

Scene 4 – AT HOME

Same scenery as Scene 1 (Step-sisters' house) Cinderella and Sisters are on stage as scene starts.

Tall Sister: Cinderella! Your sister and I are leaving for the Ball now. When we get back I want to see that the dishes are done, the floor is scrubbed, and the attic is cleaned out. Hurry along now sister or we'll be late.

Sisters exit to music. Fred enters from closet.

Cinder: Hello Fred.

Knock at door

Cinder: Come in.

Enter Fairy Godmother.

FG: Is this number 10 Garden Lane?

Cinderella nods yes.

FG: Are you Cinderella?

Cinder: Yes.

FG: Cinderella, I'm your Fairy Godmother.

Cinder: Wow!

FG: I understand that you've been making wishes. Is that right?

Cinder: Well, yes, but I didn't think they would send anyone out.

FG: You never can tell, Cinderella.

Cinder: Well I can't pay anything.

FG: It's alright, Cinderella, it's free. Who is that?

Cinder: That's my friend Fred.

FG: I see. Well, the main thing right now is to see that you get to the Prince's Ball and you can't go looking like that. We'll have to get you a new dress. You know the rules, Cinderella. Go on outside.

Cinderella exits.

FG: (*magic with wand*) Ibbity bibbity sibbity sab, ibbity bibbity canaba. All right, you can come in now, Cinderella.

Cinderella looks in mirror.

Cinder: Wow~

FG: You look just fine now. No one would ever know you in your new dress.

Cinder: But it's so late. I'll never get there on time.

FG: Do you have a horse?

Cinderella shakes head no.

FG: I could change something into a horse. But whatever I change must be alive What about Fred?

Fred runs into closet.

Cinder: (*at closet*) Fred, wouldn't you like to be a horse? Fred, wouldn't you even do it for me? Just think, Fred, you'd be a big proud horse looking over the heads of everyone and people would step back in admiration as you went by. Wouldn't you like that Fred? I think he's going to do it now, Fairy Godmother.

FG: Alright Fred, you go on outside. Ibbity bibbity sibbity sab, ibbity bibbity canaba. All right, Fred, you can come in now.

Fred looks in mirror. (Fred is now a horse)

Cinder: Oh! Fred, you're so handsome I'm sorry Fred but I think horses are supposed to stay outside.

Fred (as Horse) exits

FG: You look very pretty, Cinderella. Now hurry along and don't forget that at midnight both you and Fred will change back.

Cinder: Thank you, Fairy Godmother. Bye.

FG: Goodbye and remember that at twelve o'clock you change back.

Cinderella exits - music up - lights out - set next scene.

Scene 5 – THE PRINCE'S BALL

The stage is set with two spectators, the Sisters, the Page, and the Counselor.

Counsel: And now, in behalf of the Prince I welcome you all to the Ball and hope you have a wonderful time. Besides dancing we have some wonderful entertainment for you, and we are going to begin that entertainment at this time. First on the program we are going to be entertained by the combatants who will stage a mock battle for you. Don't be frightened, ladies. It is all in fun.

Combatants (Knights) stage battle and exit after bowing.

Counsel: Next for your enjoyment we will be entertained by a world renown musician who will play for us.

Hurdy-gurdy man plays. (mechanical piano).

Counsel: And now! For the high spot of the evening the Prince will dance the National Dance of the Kingdom with the girl chosen to be the Most Beautiful Girl at the Ball.

Prince and Cinderella dance.

Prince: And now The Most Beautiful Girl will come forward and tell us her name.

Cinder: My name is ….

Clock strikes twelve

Cinder: What time is it?

Prince: Twelve o'clock.

Cinder: Oh oh. Bye!

Prince: Come back, come back. Beautiful girl come back. Don't go away. Counselor, Counselor stop her, stop the beautiful girl Beautiful girl come back. Come back, come back, beautiful girl come back. Where are you!!!

Music up - lights out - set next scene

Scene 6 – OUTSIDE THE PALACE WALL

*Cinderella and Fred are on stage as the scene starts.
(Fred is again a mouse and Cinderella has on old clothes.)
Enter Counselor.*

Counsel: You there! Street urchin. Have you seen a beautiful girl go by here?

Cinderella shakes head no.

Counsel: (*to Fred*) and you, did you see a beautiful girl go by? Speak up!!

Cinder: He can't talk, he's a mouse.

Counsel: Oh.

Enter Prince

Prince: Did you find anyone?

Counsel: Only this street urchin.

Prince: What did she say?

Counsel: She hasn't seen anyone.

Prince: And the other one, what did he say?

Counsel: He can't talk, he's a mouse.

Prince: Oh. Look! Look what's this? Why it must be one of her shoes. The beautiful girl lost a shoe when she ran away.

Counsel: I think you're right. Yes, it is one of her shoes. I'll take it with me and look for her this way.

Exit Counsel

Prince: Beautiful girl, where are you, where are you? Beautiful girl where are you? Beautiful girl where are you?

Exit Prince

Cinder: I almost told him, but he'd never believe me. Gosh! You'd think he'd recognize me. Well, let's go home Fred.

Exit Cinderella and Fred - music up - lights out - set next scene.

Scene 7 – OFFICE

Stage has no scenery. Page and Counselor are on stage as scene begins.

Counsel: I don't know what we're goinG to do, Page. Ever since the beautiful girl ran away, the Prince has been sinking lower and lower.

Enter Prince

Counsel: Hello Prince. How are you feeling?

Prince: I'm sinking lower and lower.

Counsel: (*to Page*) See! (*back to Prince*) Prince, I thought it might cheer you up a bit if we had some entertainment so I brought someone along. Is it alright?

Prince: Yes.

Counsel: You may come up Little Margaret. Dance softly, the Prince is very sad.

Little Margaret dances.

Counsel: Feel better, Prince?

Prince: Sorry.

Counsel: I just don't know what we're going to do, Prince. We've looks and looked and looked, but we can't find the beautiful girl. I've just had an idea! Remember the beautiful girl's shoe that we found? Well, if we start and try it on every girl in the Kingdom, when we find the girl it fits, we'll have found the beautiful girl.

Prince: Wonderful! Wonderful! Wonderful!! Oh ring the bells! Let the trumpets blast! We'll find the beautiful girl at last.

Page: That rhymes.

Lights out - music up - set next scene.

Scene 8 – BACK HOME

Stage is set with Step-sister's house. No one is on stage.

Lights up - enter Tall Sister

Tall Sister: Sister! Sister! Come down quick!

Short Sister comes down stairs

Tall Sister: I just heard! Remember the shoe that the beautiful girl lost? Well, the Prince is going from house to house trying to find the one it fits and when he finds the girl it fits, he's going to marry her. Oh I'm sure it will fit me.

Short Sister: What about Cinderella. We don't want the Prince to see her.

Tall Sister: We'll hide her when the Prince comes. Oh I'm so excited.

Enter Cinderella

Tall Sister: Cinderella, have you finished chopping the wood?

Cinder: Yes.

Tall Sister: Well go look at the list, there's other things to do.

Knock at door.

Tall Sister: Oh oh. It's the Prince. We'll have to hide Cinderella. Quick!! Cinderella you get in the closet and if you know what's good for you, you won't make a sound. Now get in there.

Another knock at door - enter Prince

Prince: Page!

Enter Page (with shoe)

Prince: As you know, ladies. I am going about the Kingdom trying to find the girl that this shoe will fit and I would like to try it on you. (*toward Short Sister*) You first.

Tall Sister: No – no – no!!! Try it on me first, me first, she's too fat and ugly. You wouldn't want to marry her.

Short Sister sticks out tongue. Prince sees her.

Prince: Well! I'm sure the shoe wouldn't fit you! You are excused.

Short Sister goes upstairs. Sticks out tongue at top of stairs.

Prince: (*to Tall Sister*) Alright madam, will you please sit down and we'll try the shoe on you.

Page tries the shoe on Tall Sister.

Prince: What's the matter, Page? Madam, this is ridiculous. Your foot must be at least a size 12. It will never fit you, you are excused.

Tall Sister: I didn't want to marry you anyway!

Exit Tall Sister.

Prince: Let us go, Page.

Enter Fred to music.

Prince: Sorry, we don't try shoes on mice. What is this mouse trying to tell me? You want to shoe me something? Alright.

Prince goes to closet.

Prince: Why! There's someone in there! Whoever is in there come out.

Cinderella comes out of closet.

Prince: Why it's the beautiful girl. Come here beautiful girl. What is your name?

Cinder: My name is Cinderella. I live with my two step-sisters. They made me hide when you came.

Prince: Well, shame on them. Oh I hope the shoe fits you. Page, try the shoe on Cinderella. And push if you have to. Oh! The shoe fits, it fits. Wonderful! Everyone leave the room, I wish to speak to Cinderella alone.

Cinder: Wow!

Exit Page (door) and Fred (closet)

Prince: Cinderella, will you marry me and come and live in the Palace?

Cinder: Sure.

Prince: Cinderella, this is the happiest day of my life. Let us not tarry but leave at once.

Cinder: After you, Prince, I'm not a Princess yet.

Exit Prince.

Cinder: Goodbye old house. I hope I never see you again.

Exit Cinderella. Enter Fred (music – very sad) Fred cries.

Cinder: (*offstage*) Fred!

Enter Cinderella

Cinder: Oh Fred, I forgot. Fred, will you come and live with me in the Palace? Wonderful.

Narrator: And so it was that Cinderella married the Prince and Fred went to live with Cinderella and the Prince in the Palace and they all lived happily ever after.

Music up - exit Cinderella and Fred.

While looking through all of the Myers' documents, I was able to locate all his scripts except for Beauty and the Beast. Below is a transcript created from the audio tapes of the script.

Beauty and the Beast

Scene 1. Exterior of a Witch's house.

Narrator: Once upon a time there was a nice old lady, who was also a witch.

Witch Enters

Witch: Richard. Richard, come out of the house.

Richard Enters

Witch: Richard, I need some help. It's time to make some magic potion.

Richard: Squeaks.

Witch: I thought you would like that. Alright now, help me bring up the magic potion machine.

Witch and Richard bring up magic potion machine.

Witch: Now we'll start the fire.

Fire lights below magic potion machine.

Witch: Careful, Richard.

Witch: Oh, it's going to be a good batch, I can tell.

Richard nods his head "yes."

Witch: Listen! Oh drat, someone's coming. Go in the house, Richard.

Richard: Squeaks.

Richard Exits

Witch: I don't want anyone to find me making magic potion. It's secret!

Witch Exits. Boy enters and hits paddle ball against Witch's house.

Witch: Now cut that out!

Boy hits paddle ball against house.

Witch: You do that once more, and you're going to get it!

Boy hits paddle ball against house.

Witch: Alright, I warned you. Now I'm going to change you into something.

Raulo: Oh yeah!

Witch: Yeah.

Raulo: Oh yeah!

Witch: Yeah. I'm going to send you down, and when you come up, you are going to be something else.

Raulo: Oh yeah!

Witch: Yeah.

Boy spins off and is turned into a baby beast. Baby Beast exits.

Witch: He'll change back if he ever gets a girl to marry him. But that's not likely. Well, that's the way it goes, tiddley pom.

Witch: Richard! Richard! Wait for me! Don't drink all of the magic potion!

Witch Exits.

Scene 2. Interior of boy's house.

Mother: If Raulo doesn't get here before long he's going to miss his supper.

Father: He'll be along, Mother, he'll be along.

Mother: He knows what time we eat. Maybe he's lost in the woods.

Father: I'll send Ralph to look for him. Here Ralph! Here Ralph!

Ralph enters

Mother: Get that dog away from me!

Father: Ralph will find him.

Mother: That dumb dog couldn't find his own tail.

Father: Please, Mother, don't talk that way in front of Ralph. He's very sensitive. He's really a very smart dog. He can talk you know.

Mother looks at the audience.

Father: Say your name Ralph, say your name.

Ralph: Raulf, raulf. Raulf, raulf.

Mother: Big Deal!

Father: Not only that, but I've taught Ralph to dance.

Mother: You'd make a nice couple.

Father: No, no, Mother, he dances by himself. Watch.

Father winds phonograph four times.

Father: Now remember. One, two three. One, two three. Understand?

Ralph nods "yes." Ralph dances.

Father: Alright, Ralph. Go find Raulo, go find Raulo.

Ralph exits.

Father: Ralph had probably treed a cat.

Mother: Or vica versa.

Ralph enters loudly whimpering.

Mother: Well, what's the matter with man's best friend?

Baby Beast enters.

Father: Great heavens, Mother. What's happened to Raulo? Why our son has turned into a little beast!

Mother: Come here, Raulo. Whatever has happened to you? Why, he can't even talk. Whatever are we going to do?

Father: Well, I know it is going to be difficult, Mother. But we'll have to raise him just as though he were a normal little boy.

Mother: Alright. Raulo, go wash your paws. They're filthy.

Baby Beast exits.

Mother: Oh, this is a sad day!

Father: Yes, Mother, a sad, sad day. Uh, pass the potatoes.

Scene 3. Years Later.

Narrator: Time passed, and the Beast grew up.

Father: This is going to be a hard thing to do, but it must be done. Raulo, Raulo, come here.

Beast Enters.

Father: Raulo, you're a grown beast now. And your Mother and I have decided that it is time for you to go out into the world and make your own way.

Mother: That's right, Raulo.

Father: Your Mother has made you a bag of peanut butter sandwiches to take with you.

Beast grabs the bag of sandwiches.

Father: You may listen to one record before your go.

Beast winds the record player. Sad music plays.

Father: Take care.

Mother: Write if you get work.

Beast exits with his bag of Sandwiches.

Mother: This is the saddest day of our lives.

Father: It certainly is, Mother. It certainly is. Uh, pass the oregano.

Scene 4. Guard Post

Tall Guard: Spatkauf, Spatkauf. Are you in there?

Short Guard: Duh, hi!

Tall Guard: I've come to relieve you.

Short Guard: *(To Audience)* I'm relieved.

Tall Guard: How are things out here?

Short Guard: As usual. Duh, how are things back at the palace?

Tall Guard: As usual. I thought if you have the time, we might practice our fast drill.

Short Guard: Duh, our fast drill? Duh, sure, I got the time. I need the practice.

Tall Guard: Are you ready?

Short Guard: Duh, oh, I'm ready.

Tall Guard: Here we go.

The Guards perform their marching routine, messing up here and there.

Short Guard: Duh, I need more practice.

Tall Guard: We need more practice….Listen, what's that? Go look.

Short Guard: Duh, I'm off duty.

Tall Guard: I'll bet it's a lion.

Short Guard: Duh, at least a lion!

Tall Guard: Hey, you there! Come Out!

Beast enters from behind rocks.

Tall Guard: Stand there.

Short Guard: Yoink! It's a Beast! Duh, Boy! Wait till we show the King! Duh, be careful! There might be another one back there.

Tall Guard: No, there's only a bag of peanut butter sandwiches.

Short Guard: I'll go ahead and tell the King we're coming.

Short Guard exits.

Tall Guard: Alright you! Step smartly.

Tall Guard and Beast exit.

Scene 5. Inside Palace

Jester enters.

King: Jester, what sort of entertainment do you have for us today?

Jester: Today, King, we have a most talented musician. Baby William will play the xylophone.

Baby William plays the xylophone.

King: Uh, that kid is great! Anything else?

Jester: Yes, we have a juggler who will perform for us.

Juggler enters. First balancing a ball on his nose, then spinning a plate on a pole, and lastly balancing a chair on the pole.

King: We ought to have him here to balance our budget! Ah Ha Ha Ha!

Son: (*To audience*) My Father, the King!

Knock at Door.

King: Jester, go open the door.

Jester exits. Short Guard enters.

Short Guard: Duh, King. Duh, we just captured the Beast outside of the Palace grounds.

King: Well have him brought in.

Short Guard: Duh, alright King.

Short Guard exits. Tall Guard and Beast enter.

Daughter: Oh, he's awful! Blah!

Son: He's gross!

King: Guard, did the Beast have anything with him when he was captured?

Guard: A bag of peanut butter sandwiches.

King: (*to audience*) He can't be all bad. (*To guard*) Guard, take the Beast to the dungeon.

Tall Guard and Beast Exit.

Daughter: Daddy, can I go over to Sally's and play tennis?

King: Yes, Daughter.

Daughter exits.

Son: Dad, can I go over to Rowland's and play in the dungeon?

King: Yes, Son.

Son exits.

King: Geraldine, what are you going to do? Why don't you play with your brother and sister?

Geraldine: They don't want me to play with them. They don't like me. No one wants to play with me.

King: I just don't understand you, Geraldine. Well, I have to go, bye.

King exits.

Geraldine: No one wants to play with me. (*Looks off stage left*) Guard!

Tall Guard enters

Geraldine: Guard, bring out the Beast.

Tall Guard: Oh, I don't think your father would like that. Don't you forget, your father is a King.

Geraldine: And don't you forget that I'm a Princess. Now, bring up the Beast!

Tall Guard: Yes, Princess Geraldine.

Tall Guard exits. Tall Guard and Beast enter.

Tall Guard: I'll stand here.

Geraldine: You'll stand elsewhere!

Tall Guard: Yes, Princess.

Tall Guard exits.

Geraldine: Do you understand when I talk to you?

Beast nods "yes".

Geraldine: But you can't talk?

Beast nods "no".

Geraldine: Do you know how to play bounce ball?

Beast nods "no".

Geraldine: (*To Audience*) Maybe he doesn't know how to play any games.

(*To Beast*) Haven't you ever had anyone to play with?

Beast nods "no".

Geraldine: Poor thing.

Geraldine bounces the ball.

Geraldine: Do you think you can do that?

Geraldine and Beast bounce the ball back and forth.

Geraldine: (*to the audience*) He learns fast. (*to Beast*) Do you know how to dance?

Beast nods "no".

Geraldine: Watch.

Geraldine dances.

Geraldine: Now you try it.

Beast clumsily fails to dance.

Geraldine: Maybe you'd better not try any more today.

Beast enthusiastically nods "yes."

Geraldine: I like his spirit.

Beast attempts to dance again…this time more gracefully. The dance evolves into a waltz by Beast and Geraldine.

Geraldine dances off and returns sitting with a ball.

Geraldine: Beast, the ball rolled out into the garden. Would you go get it?

Beast exits and returns sits.

Geraldine: Thank you, Beast. Now give me the ball.

Beast looks at Geraldine, then back to the audience.

Geraldine: Please, give me the ball. Beast, if you don't give me the ball, I'm going to be mad! Now give it to me!

Beast shows Geraldine a flower.

Geraldine: Aw.

Scene 6 The Palace Days Later.

King: Where is Princess Geraldine?

Daughter: Aw, Daddy. She is out with the Beast picking wild flowers.

King: Very well, we'll proceed without her. Jester, what sort of entertainment do you have for us today? Every day's the same around here.

Jester: First on the program, we're going to have a trapeze artist.

Trapeze artist enters and performs his aerial act then exits.

Jester: And next....

King: I hope it's something quiet.

Jester: And next, we are to be entertained by a wonderful guitarist.

Guitar player enters and performs, then exits.

King: Jester, go find Princess Geraldine and the Beast and send them in.

Jester exits.

Daughter: Oh Daddy, do we have to have the Beast in here?

King: It's alright Daughter, the Beast seems quite harmless. And Geraldine likes to play with him.

Daughter: Well, I don't like him. He's dumb.

Son: Yeah Dumb!

Geraldine and Beast enter.

Son: Geraldine likes the Beast. Geraldine likes the Beast. Geraldine likes the Beast. She'd probably marry him if she could.

Geraldine: Yes I would!

Beast spins off and is replaced by a tall tennis player named Raulo.

Raulo: Tennis anyone?

Geraldine: (*To audience*) Brother!

Daughter: The Beast changed into a handsome man! He's cute!

Son: He's great!

King: Come forward, sir, and tell us how you came to be here.

Raulo: My name is Raulo, Your Majesty, and I don't know how I got here.

King: Well, we are most fortunate to have a handsome fellow like you here in our court. We would like you to stay with us.

Raulo: Oh, thank you, your Majesty. That would be jolly!

Daughter: Raulo, would you like to come over to Sally's with me and play tennis?

Raulo: Love to.

Son: And later, would you like to come over to Rowland's with me and play in the dungeon?

Raulo: Love to.

Geraldine: And would you like to play bounce-ball with me?

Raulo: Please, now that I'm a handsome man, I cannot be bothered playing children's games. Really!

Daughter: Come along Raulo.

Daughter exits.

Raulo: Be right there! Ta, Ta, everyone!

Raulo exits.

Geraldine: Geesh!

Son: I'm going too dad.

Son exits.

Geraldine: It's not fair, Papa! I'm the one who looked after him and took care of him. Oh, what am I gonna do?

King: I'm sorry, Geraldine, but you're a big girl now and you'll have to figure things out for yourself. Well, I gotta go now, bye.

King exits.

Geraldine: Oh, what am I gonna do?

King: (*Voice*) You're a big girl now Geraldine, and you'll have to figure things out for yourself.

Geraldine: I know. I'll run away!

Geraldine exits.

Scene 7. Outside Witch's house

Witch: Leaves gotta fall. Fish gotta swim. Birds gotta fly. (*to audience*) That's the way it goes, tiddley pom.

Witch dances.

Witch: Oh Richard, how we danced when I was young. And the things we did!

Richard squeaks

Witch: Even that!

Richard: (*To audience*) Wow!

Witch: Shhh. Someone's coming.

Geraldine enters.

Witch: There, there, doll, what's your name and what's your problem?

Geraldine: My name is Geraldine and my problem is that my best friend doesn't like me anymore.

Witch: Oh, that's too bad. How did all this happen?

Geraldine: Well, one day, when my brother and sister were teasing me, they said "you'd probably marry him if you could." And I said "yes." And then all of a sudden he changed into a man.

Witch: You mean that before that he wasn't a man?

Geraldine: Well, no. He was a Beast. He was a most kind and gentle beast. And we used to play bounce-ball and pick wild flowers together. And now that he's a man, he doesn't like me anymore.

Witch: You mean, that as a Beast he was kind and gentle, but as a man he...

Geraldine: He was (*makes a raspberry sound*).

Witch: Don't be rude, Geraldine!

Geraldine: I can't help it. He just turned into a big nothing! A dinga-ling!

Richard pantomimes the boy turning into a Beast.

Witch: Great Scott, Richard, you're right. It happened so long ago that I'd forgotten. Geraldine, I'm the one who turned him into a Beast in the first place.

Geraldine: Gosh! You must be a Witch!

Witch: You'd better believe it.

Geraldine: I do, I do. Well, then, would you do me a favor and change him back into a Beast?

Witch: Well, I'm not sure I can. Wait a minute.

Witch exits and returns with a Farmer's Almanac.

Witch: Now, let's see. Let's see, let's see. Between the 21st and the 27th, full moon, uh, good time for planting corn. (*To Richard*) I must remember that. (*Back to book*) Ah, here it is. Here. Very simple, very sim...

Witch: All you have to do is to get him to kiss you and he will change back into a Beast.

Geraldine: But, how will I do that? He doesn't like me!

Witch: You are a big girl now, Geraldine, and you'll have to figure things out for yourself. Well, I got to go now, bye. Come on, Richard.

Witch and Richard exit.

Geraldine: Oh, what am I going to do? What am I going to do?

Witch: (*Voice*) Geraldine, you're a big girl now, and you will have to...

Geraldine: Oh, knock it off!

Geraldine exits.

Scene 8. The Palace

King: Are we all ready to go?

Daughter: Yes, Daddy.

King: Son, you run ahead and see if the carriage is ready.

Son exits.

King: Geraldine,

King: Geraldine, we're going now. You take care of things here at the palace and we'll bring you something when we come back. Is there anything you want before we go?

Geraldine whispers in King's ear.

King: What!

Geraldine again whispers.

King: *(To Geraldine)* You want Raulo to kiss you!

Geraldine: Aw, Papa, you don't have to talk so loud.

Daughter: Oh, Daddy, please don't embarrass Raulo!

King: No, we must remember that Geraldine was nice to Raulo when he was a Beast. And besides, it can't hurt anything. Raulo, kiss Geraldine goodbye.

Raulo kisses Geraldine then spins off stage and returns as Beast.

Daughter: Yuck, he's changed back into the Beast!

King: Not very constant, is he.

Daughter: Well, he's not going with us, that's for sure. Let's go, Daddy, we'll be late.

Daughter exits.

King: Good-bye, Geraldine. Take good care of the place.

King exits.

Geraldine: He's back!

Beast and Geraldine dance off stage.
Geraldine returns and performs a ballet.
After the Ballet, she exits. Geraldine and the Beast return sitting.

Geraldine: Are you glad to be back?

Beast shakes head "yes."

Geraldine: I'm glad too.

Beast reaches up to hand Geraldine the flower.

Narrator: And so it was that once again, Geraldine had her friend. And they all lived happily ever after.

Music up - The End

Simple Simon

"Simple Simon" is the story of a boy (young man) who wants to be a juggler and an acrobat.

It is also the story of an orphan girl named "Marianna" who works for the bad man and wife who run (operate) the Fair.

Scene 1. SIMON'S HOME

Simon breaks many things practicing to be a juggler. His father and mother suggest that he go to the Fair where he might get a job as an apprentice juggler and acrobat. Simon and his friend (Walter the chicken) leave for the Fair.

Scene 2. FIRST DAY OF THE FAIR

Simon and Walter (the chicken) have not arrived at the Fair as yet. We meet Mariamne and the bad man and wife. We watch the Acts of the Fair: two acrobats, a dancer, and a juggler.

Scene 3. ON THE WAY TO THE FAIR

Simon and Walter meet a Pieman.Scene

4. SECOND DAY OF THE FAIR

Simon and Walter have arrived at the Fair. We watch the Acts of the Fair: boxers, Baby William at the accordion, and Mariamne riding the wheel. After dark (at night) Simon and Walter sneak back to the Fair to practice on the rope (tight rope). They meet Mariamne. They discover that the bad man and wife are going to do something bad to Mariamne. Simon, Mariamne and Walter run away to the hills.

Scene 5. NIGHT IN THE HILLS

Simon and Mariamne practice an acrobat act to perform next day at the Fair, which is King's Day at the Fair. If they win the contest, all will be good for Mariamne.

Scene 6. KING'S DAY AT THE FAIR

We watch the Acts of the Fair: acrobat, dancers and Baby William at the violin. King allows Simon and Mariamne to perform and they win. We find the Pieman was the King in disguise.

Scene 1. SIMON'S HOME

Bare stage except for Simon's Mother and Father rocking in rocking chairs.
There is a small set piece on stage. An offstage door slams and Simon runs in with a ball balanced on his nose.

Simon: Hey, Mom! Hey, Dad! Watch me balance the ball. Watch me! Watch me! Ooph! (*Simon stumbles, falls, and disappears.*)

Mother: I don't know what we are going to do about Simon. All he thinks about is becoming a juggler or an acrobat.

Father: A-ah .. A-ah (*yes .. yes*)

They rock. The door slams again.
Simon enters balancing some dishes on a pole.

Simon: Hey, Mom! Hey, Dad! Watch this! Watch! Ooph! (*Crash as he stumbles, falls, and disappears.*)

Mother: We have to get Simon out of here before he breaks up everything in the house.

Father: A-ah .. A-ah. I'm sorry, Mother, I think Simon is simple. (*spells out*) s-i-m-p-l-e.

Mother: I'm afraid so. All our hopes.

Father: All our plans.

Mother: Down the drain

Father: A-ah .. A-ah.

Door slams and Simon enters.

Simon: Hey, Mom! Hey, Dad! Watch this! I'm going to jump .. I'm going to jump .. Watch!

Simon hits the wall, falls back and disappears.

Mother: All day long it's smash, crash … smash, crash.

Father: A-ah.

Door slams again and Simon enters with Walter the chicken.

Simon: Hey, Mom! Hey, Dad! Watch what Walter can do. Watch!

Mother: I've seen what Walter can do. Now get that chicken out of the house.

Father: Wait a minute, Mother. Simon, if you want to be an acrobat so bad, why don't you and Walter go to the Fair and watch the acrobats.

Simon: It's too late. The Fair starts today. We wouldn't get there until tomorrow.

Father: A-ah, but the Fair last three days so you'd still be there for the last two days.

Simon: You mean you wouldn't mind if Walter and I left?

Father: Not at all.

Mother: NOT AT ALL!

Father: In Fact, Simon, you might get a job as an apprentice acrobat.

Simon: Wow! Walter, let's go! Bye.

Father: Bye.

Mother: Bye. Come home for Christmas.

Simon and Walter leave for the Fair.

Mother: Ah, peace.

Father: Peace.

They rock for a bit.

Mother: I should have made that Easter.

Father: A-ah ... a-ah.

Lights down

Scene 2. FIRST DAY OF THE FAIR

Sound of clomping down stair then Bad Woman enters.

Bad Woman: Melvin!

A mean dog sticks his head up.

Bad Woman: Melvin! Go get Mariamne.

Melvin exits then returns with Mariamne.

Mariamne: You rang?

Bad Woman: Don't get smart with me. Have you cleaned up backstage?

Mariamne: No.

Bad Woman: Well don't just stand there, dummy. Go do it. The Fair is about to start.

Bad Woman disappears then sound of stomping upstairs. Mariamne goes behind the curtain on the stage, Melvin stays on stage. Moises as Mariamne cleans up. Bad Woman enters after clomping down stairs.

Bad Woman: Mariamne, are you finished yet?

Mariamne: (*offstage*) Yes.

Bad Woman: I don't believe it. I'm coming back.

Bad Woman sticks her head behind the curtain on the little stage.

Bad Woman: You call that clean? It's terrible. Come out here!

Mariamne comes out and they go down to front of main stage.

Bad Woman: Listen, dummy, if you can't clean up better than that, we'll send you back where you came from.

Mariamne: NO! NO! Please don't send me back! Please don't send me back!

Bad Woman: Well then, "shape up" dummy or back you go. Now get under the stage where you belong.

Mariamne goes under the stage.

Bad Woman: Melvin! See that she stays under the stage.

Melvin goes under the stage.

Mariamne: (*pops up quickly*) I hate that dog!

Bad Woman goes to the stairway and calls up.

Bad Woman: Husband! Are you coming down or aren't you. The Fair is about to start and you're still up there fiddling around.

Crowd noises as the audience arrives. Bad Woman goes back to stairway.

Bad Woman: WILL YOU HURRY UP! The crowd is here.

Bad Man stomps down stairs and appears.

Bad Man: I'm here, sweetheart.

Bad Woman: So is the plague. I'm going upstairs and watch from the window.

She exits and clomps up the stairs.

Bad Man: Hey hey hey hey! May I have your complete attention. It's time to start the Fair, and here to officially open the Fair is Baby William at the bass drum. (*He looks around*) Where's that kid? Get that kid up here.

Baby William plays the drum and marches around.

Bad Man: And now the first act of the day. (*He puts up the teeter totter.*) May I now introduce you to the Twickanham Twins – Albrecht and Elmer. Are you fellas ready? (*He listens at the curtain*)

Hey hey hey hey, they're ready. First we give you Albrecht and then Elmer. Hey hey hey hey, let's go!

Bad Man exits. Teeter totter act and Bad Man returns.

Bad Man: Next on the program … Little Ingrid will dance for you. (*He puts up a dance platform*) Are you ready Little Ingrid? She's ready. Hey hey hey hey, let's go.

Bad Man exits, Little Ingrid dances.

At the end of her dance the Bad Man puts up the balls for the juggler.

Bad Man: And now to end the first day at the Fair we present Pierrot! Are you ready Pierrot? He's ready so … Hey hey hey hey, let's go.

Bad Man exits, Pierrot does his juggling and dance act then the Bad Man returns.

Bad Man: That's all for today, folks. Hurry back again tomorrow. Same place, same time.

Bad Man stomps upstairs, the crowd disappears, and Bad Woman clomps down stairs.

Bad Woman: Melvin! (*Melvin comes out*) Melvin go get Mariamne. (Mariamne comes up) Mariamne I want you to clean up the place, right now.

Mariamne: But I haven't had anything to eat yet.

Bad Woman: Tough luck, dummy. Melvin! See that Mariamne does her work AND DOESN'T RUN AWAY.

Bad Woman clomps upstairs and Melvin growls.

Mariamne: I hate that dog.

*Mariamne disappears under the stage.
Melvin growls, looks around, then sinks out of sight. Lights down.*

Scene 3. ON THE WAY TO THE FAIR

*The stage is bare save for a sign pointing to the Fair.
An old man enters. He carries a case of pies on his back.*

Pieman: I'm getting too old for this. (*He puts down the pies.*) I think I'll take a nap. (*He lies down to sleep. Simon and Walter enter and see the Pieman.*)

Simon: We've got to hurry, Walter. We're already a day late for the Fair.

Pieman: (*wakes up*) Hello young fella. Hello chicken.

Simon: My name is Simon and this is Walter. We're on our way to the Fair.

Pieman: So am I. We're a day late, you know. If I don't get there soon, I may as well give my pies to the birds (*He looks at Walter*) No offence, Walter.

Simon: I'm going to the Fair to watch the acrobats. That's what I want to do, I want to be an acrobat.

Pieman: If that's what you want to do, you'll have to practice, practice, practice.

Simon: I've been practicing. Watch. Stand back, Walter

Simon walks on his hands.

Pieman: Fine Simon, fine. Keep up the good work. Well I suppose we'd better be getting on.0

Simon: Can we help you carry the pies?

Pieman: No thanks. "sic transit Gloria mundi"

Simon: What's that mean?

Pieman: You win some and you lose some.

Simon: Well bye. See you at the Fair. Come on Walter.

Pieman: (to the audience) Bye. Nice kids. Chow.

Scene 4. SECOND DAY OF THE FAIR

The crowd, Simon and Walter are on stage.
The Bad Man stomps downstairs.

Bad Man: Hey hey hey hey. May I have your attention! It is time to start things off for the second day at the Fair. We have more great acts for you, and I see some new faces an ah (*looks at Walter*) Sorry, no chickens allowed. NO CHICKENS ALLLOWED!

Simon: Wait outside for me, Walter. (*Walter exits*)

Bad Man: And now for the first act of the day. We're going to have a boxing batch with the McDougall Twins ... Raoual and Irvin. (*Bad Man mumbles about the rules to the boxers*) They know the rules so hey hey hey hey, let's go!

The boxers fight and end up doing a silly dance.

Bad Man: Next for your enjoyment we present Baby William at the accordion. Where's that kid? Get that kid up here.

Baby William plays the accordion.

Bad Man: And now for the last act of the day our own dear, sweet Mariamne will ride the wheel for you.

Mariamne rides the unicycle.

Bad Man: That ends things for today but, hey hey hey hey, don't forget tomorrow is KING'S DAY AT THE FAIR. The last and most important day of all. Hey hey hey hey.

Bad Man exist and Bad Woman comes down stairs.

Bad Woman: Melvin. Melvin, go get Mariamne.

Mariamne comes up.

Bad Woman: What were you trying to do? Show everyone how bad you can ride the wheel?

Mariamne: I thought I was pretty good.

Bad Woman: DON"T TALK BACK TO ME, DUMMY. Just for that you can go to bed without your supper. Now get under the stage where you belong. Melvin, see that she stays there.

Mariamne and Melvin go down. Bad Woman goes to the stairway and yells.

Bad Woman: (*to husband*) Hey! Let's go.

Bad Man comes down and they exit.

Lights are lowered to night scene.

Scene 4 (part 2)

Stage is empty. The tight rope where Mariamne rode her unicycle is still up. Simon and Walter sneak back to the Fair to practice on the tight rope.

Simon: Hey, Great! They left up the rope I'll try.

Walter jumps up and down.

Simon: You want to try it first? Okay.

Walter does his act on the rope.

Simon: That was great, Walter. Now I'll try it. HEY WAIT! There's something under the stage.

Simon goes under the stage and comes back up with Mariamne.

Simon: Why, it's the girl that rode the wheel. I'm Simon, and this is Walter.

Mariamne: I'm Mariamne.

Simon: What are you doing under there?

Mariamne: The people I work for make me stay under there.

Simon: Boy! If they made me stay under there, I'd quit.

Mariamne: I can't quit. If I quit, they'd send me back where I came from and I don't want to go back there. It's terrible. I saw you when I rode the wheel. Why did you come back?

Simon: To see if I could walk the rope. I want to be an acrobat.

Mariamne: No kidding. Hey, I'll help you. I'm a good acrobat. Watch.

Mariamne does her little walk on the rope.

Mariamne: Now you try it.

Simon tries to walk the rope and falls off a lot.

Mariamne: Say, you've got talent. All you need is practice.

Simon: Thanks. But you're the one that's good.

Mariamne: That's true, Simon, but you must remember, I'm a pro. I'd better take down the rope.

She takes down rope and Melvin comes up.

Simon: WHAT"S THAT?

Mariamne: Oh, that's Melvin. He's the meanest dog in town. He belongs to the people I work for. They think if they keep a mean dog around it will keep me from running away.

Simon: Does it?

Mariamne: You'd better believe it!

Simon: What's it like under there?

Mariamne: It's terrible. Con on, I'll show you.

Simon and Mariamne exit. Walter is still on stage to one side. Enter Bad Man and Bad Woman.

Bad Woman: Let's get something straight right now. I don't want Mariamne around here after tomorrow. She has to go.

Bad Man: Alright, alright. Tomorrow we'll send her back where she came from.

Bad Woman: She nothing but a dumb, dumb dummy.

Bad Man: Say, that's catchy. Dun, dun dummy. Dun, dun, dummy.

Bad Woman: Shut up! Come on.

Bad Man and Bad Woman go upstairs. Sounds of them brushing their teeth and getting into bed. Mariamne and Simon return.

Simon: Boy! That's terrible under there.

Walter, in pantomime, tells Simon he has heard the Bad Man and Bad Woman say tomorrow they will send Mariamne back where she came from.

Simon: Don't worry, Mariamne. We'll protect you. We'll run away.

Mariamne: We can't run away. Melvin will get us.

Melvin comes up and Walter chases him away.

Mariamne: Thank you, Walter.

Simon: Walter may be a chicken but he's no coward. Come on! Let's get out of here before Melvin comes back.

Exit Simon, Mariamne and Walter.

Scene 5. NIGHT IN THE HILLS

Simon, Mariamne and Walter have run off to the mountains. It is night, the moon is out. The stage is bare except for the mountain-type scenery. Enter Simon, Mariamne and Walter. Walter pecks around and disappears.

Simon: They won't find us here. You rest, I'll gather some wood and make a fire. Don't wander off, Walter.

Simon makes a fire – Mariamne is sitting down,

Mariamne: You build a good fire.

Simon: Thanks.

Mariamne: You know tomorrow is King's Day at the Fair – the day the King comes to watch the acts and pick the best one. If you win, you're famous. Simon, if we could do an act and win, the people I work for wouldn't dare send me back.

Simon: You could ride the wheel. That was good.

Mariamne: No, Simon, that's too easy. It has to be something hard. Something like a pole balancing act.

Simon: What's that?

Mariamne: Well, one person holds a long pole and the other person balances on top of it. It's very hard.

Simon: There's a limb over there. We could try it.

Mariamne: Okay.

Simon and Mariamne do their balancing act. They disappear at end and come back as sitting puppets.

Mariamne: That was great! We're going to win, we're going to win! You were really great, Simon. But if we go back to the Fair, the bad people will see us.

Simon: We could stay hidden until it was time for the act.

Mariamne: Okay.

Walter comes in but stays at edge of stage.

Mariamne: It is nice here by the fire. (*She notices Walter*) Why don't you ask Walter to come over by the fire.

Simon: Walter, would you like to come over by the fire with us?

Walter comes over and sits down. Mariamne looks at Simon and Walter.

Mariamne: It must be nice to have a family.

Scene 6. KING'S DAY AT THE FAIR

Enter Guard.

Guard: All hail! All hail! The King approaches. Here comes the King

King enters.

195

King: I hereby proclaim this day to be King's Day at the Fair. Let's get this show on the road.

Guard: Ok, King. The first act will be Roger the Acrobat with little Ingrid assisting. Are you ready? They're ready.

Roger does his act.

Guard: Next we have a dance team.

The Bad Man and Bad Woman dance.

Guard: And now for the last act, we have Baby William at the Violin. Where's that kid?

Baby William plays.

King: Thank you one and all. And now I will choose the winner. I choose….

Simon rushes in

Simon: WAIT! WAIT! PLEASE WAIT!

Guard: You're too late, you're too late. It's all over.

King: One minute, Guard.

Guard: But it's too late.

King: Quiet. Now then, go ahead

Simon: Come in Mariamne. Mariamne and I want to perform for you.

Guard: But it's against the rules.

King: WILL YOU KEEP QUIET! Go ahead with your act.

Simon and Mariamne do the balancing act with Walter at the top.

King: That was top drawer. You win. Simon and Mariamne win.

Someone in Crowd: The King knew his name!

Simon: He knew my name.

King: That's right, Simon. Sometimes I put on a disguise and go out among my people to see what's going on. Simon, I met you the day before yesterday.

Simon: I don't remember. The only person I met was … the Pieman!

King: That's right, Simon. I was the Pieman.

Simon: CRIPA DODDLE!

Enter Bad Woman who stops beside Mariamne.

Bad Woman: THERE SHE IS! You dumb, dumb dummy. Listen you little dummy, you ran away and now you're going to get it.

Enter Bad Man

Bad Man: Did you find her? Boy! Is she going to get it!

King: Mariamne, who are these people?

Bad Woman and Bad Man: Oh oh, she's knows the King!

King: Who are these people, Mariamne?

Mariamne: There are the bad people I work for. They made me sleep under the stage.

Simon: Yes, and they were going to send her back to some terrible place and she didn't want to go.

King: Is this true?

Bad Woman: (*stutters*) Well … I … err …well…

King: Stow it. I've got the picture. Go, you bad people and don't come back!!

Simon whispers to King

King: And Simon says Take your dumb dog with you!

Melvin runs out, Mariamne makes a rude noise.

King: I like her spunk. Thank you all for coming. And now the Fair is all over and you all can go home. You two stick around. You too, Walter.

Crowd disappears

King: Where are you two going?

Simon: We don't know.

King: Well, I've been thinking about you kids. There's not much going on around the palace these days. Why don't you all come home with me. It would liven things up a bit. Come on, Walter. You two hurry along, you hear?

Simon and Mariamne do a dance and stand at the end.

Narrator: And so it was that when they were a little older, Simon and Mariamne got married, and Simon became counselor to the King, and Walter was appointed head chicken, and they all lived happily ever after.

www.ingramcontent.com/pod-product-compliance
Lightning Source LLC
Chambersburg PA
CBHW060512300426
44112CB00017B/2635